TEXAS, HER TEXAS

The Life and Times of Frances Goff

TEXAS, HER TEXAS

The Life and Times of Frances Goff

NANCY BECK YOUNG
AND
LEWIS L. GOULD

PREFACE BY ANN W. RICHARDS

Published for the Center for American History
by the Texas State Historical Association
Austin

Library of Congress Cataloging-in-Publication Data:
Young, Nancy Beck
    Texas, her Texas : The life and times of Frances Goff / Nancy Beck Young, Lewis L. Gould : preface by Ann W. Richards.
        p.   cm. — (Barker Texas History Center series : no. 6)
        Includes bibliographical references and index
        ISBN 0-87611-159-2 (alk. paper)
        1. Goff, Frances, 1916–1994.   2. Texas—Biography.   3. Texas—Politics and Government—1951– .   4. University of Texas M. D. Anderson Cancer Center. 5. Women—Texas—Societies and clubs—History—20th century. I. Gould, Lewis L. II. University of Texas at Austin. Center for American History.   III. Title.
IV. Series: Barker Texas History Center series (Texas State Historical Association) ; no. 6.
        CT275.G5527Y68   1997
        976.4'063'092—dc21
                                        96–52778
                                            CIP
5   4   3   2   1   97 98 99 00 01

Published for the Center for American History by the Texas State Historical Association in cooperation with the Center for Studies in Texas History at the University of Texas at Austin.

Number six in the Barker Texas History Center Series
Senior Editor, Don E. Carleton

Book design by William V. Bishel. Dustjacket design by David Timmons.

∞The paper used in this book meets the minimum requirements of the American National Standard for Permanence of Paper for Printed Library Materials, z39.84—1984.

This book was made possible in part by grants from the M. D. Anderson Foundation, Houston; the Littlefield Fund for Southern History, the University of Texas at Austin; and the Powell Foundation, Houston.

Frontispiece: Frances Goff with background of photographs on wall. Photographs depict, from left to right and top to bottom: Laura Lou Coffey, Mary Ann Wycoff, Sara Speights, Brenda Cook, Jeff Rasco, Wanda Sumrall, Marilynn Wood, Judy Shields, Minnie Lyle, Anne Hodges and Rubyrae Foster, and Bea Ann Smith. *CN 08982. Courtesy Frances Goff Papers, Center for American History, University of Texas at Austin.*

Contents

Preface

Frances Goff had an enormous influence on my life. To explain in exactly what ways is difficult. It is sort of like saying, "How did your mother influence you?" That's why I am so pleased that Nancy Beck Young and Lewis Gould have written this book on her life.

I thought I knew a lot about Frances until I read this book. Frances did great things, but she also did thousands of small things every day that improved people's lives. The measure of a person often comes down to the details of that person's life. So it is with Frances. This book does the difficult job of laying out those details.

When I was first chosen to go to Girls State, it was really quite a thing for me. I was a country girl who had moved to the big city of Waco. Frances was the dominant person in my life during the time I was at Girls State, from my first year on. In those days, with Frances, we always felt as if the tally sheet was not quite in on us yet. There was always one more hill to climb, one more test to pass. So when I was chosen to go to Girls Nation I was pleased. I don't know whether I was as pleased about winning a trip to Washington as I was about having Frances's approval.

At that time there were very few women who were really players in the political world. We would go to Girls State early, and do menial work before the program began. One day we needed something and we couldn't get it. I think it had something to do with bedframes. Frances said: "You tell those people if we don't have those here this afternoon, I will call Emma Long." Emma Long was on the city council in Austin, and whatever it was that the city was not doing that Frances thought they ought to do, she was going to sic Emma Long on them. It made a profound impression on me that Emma Long had that kind of authority.

I've been back and spoken to the girls now for about fourteen years. Frances wanted any woman who was elected to come. I think she knew that these girls get an idea about what they can aspire to be only through seeing women in roles of authority, very much like I sat there awed by Allan Shivers and John Ben Shepperd and Price Daniel. It was just this great joy and pride that she had, this grand lioness of a woman, who nurtured and judged these kids out of the pack, and they had survived and done well.

I stayed in touch with Frances only sporadically over the years when she was doing so much to build the nation's best cancer center, M. D. Anderson. In my governor's race, though, Frances was hands-on. It was simply amazing. She raised money. She brought me to meet people and them to meet me. She did a great job.

Frances, to me, was like the base, she was the shoulders to stand on. You knew that no matter what you might ask of her, within reason she would do it. She was a constant support system. In some ways, Frances was a lot like my mother. Nothing you ever did would quite be good enough. So in that sense, she kept you on your toes. But she was one of the really serious encouraging people I had in my life. I never have known what the word leadership means. I know what a leader is when I see one, but I don't necessarily know what the attributes are because they vary. But Frances taught me something about leadership. It was that if you have a position, if you have a belief, you have an obligation to express it, you owe something to your country. She was fiercely patriotic. The sense of responsibility and obligation was very much in Frances's vocabulary. She translated that to all of us. We had to do it. We owed it to our neighbors, our community, our country. This fine book is an excellent tribute to a great woman who had the courage to reach for the stars at a time when reaching beyond boundaries was not a path women were supposed to take.

Ann W. Richards

Foreword

Texas, Her Texas: The Life and Times of Frances Goff is the sixth volume in the Barker Texas History Center Series, a cooperative publication program of the University of Texas at Austin Center for American History (CAH) and the Texas State Historical Association (TSHA). CAH is a special collections library, archive, and museum that facilitates research and sponsors programs on the historical development of the United States. Its components include the Barker Texas History Collections, the Sam Rayburn Library and Museum (in Bonham, Texas), Winedale Historical Center (near Round Top, Texas), the Littlefield Southern History Collections, and the Congressional History Collections. CAH supports research and education by acquiring, preserving, and making accessible research collections and by sponsoring exhibitions, conferences, symposia, oral history projects, publications, fellowships, and grant-funded initiatives. Its research collection strengths include the history of Texas, the South, the Southwest, and the Rocky Mountain West.

CAH and TSHA established the Barker series to encourage and support the publication of historical studies based mainly on the Center's Barker Texas History Collections, which includes the nation's largest library of Texana as well as extensive holdings of archival, cartographic, newspaper, sound, and photographic material. Texas, Her Texas: The Life and Times of Frances Goff was selected to appear as a volume in the Barker series because a significant portion of the book is based on research conducted by the authors in two CAH collections: the Frances Goff Papers and the historical archive of the Bluebonnet Girls State Program. Donated to the CAH in 1994, the Goff papers and the Girls State archive are valuable additions to our holdings on women's history. An important supplement to these collections are the oral history interviews that Lewis Gould and Nancy Beck Young conducted during their research for this book. Professors Gould and Young worked closely with CAH Associate Director Katherine Adams to insure that the Goff Papers, the Girls State archive, and the oral history tapes were brought together and placed at the CAH. Thanks to them, these collections will bene-fit future researchers interested in a wide variety of topics associated with the work of Frances Goff and the activities of Girls State.

For a period of many decades now, the collaboration between CAH and TSHA has resulted in significant contributions to our knowledge about the historical development of Texas. TSHA Director Ron Tyler and Assistant Director George Ward were enthusiastically supportive of this project from its earliest stages. I thank them, their talented staff, and the Association's Executive Council for making possible the publication of *Texas, Her Texas: The Life and Times of Frances Goff.*

> Don E. Carleton, Director
> Center for American History

Introduction

This book began in the autumn of 1992 when Anne Hodges Morgan convinced Frances Goff that an oral history project about her career would be a worthwhile endeavor. Out of those discussions came the project at the University of Texas at Austin to record a series of interviews with Frances covering her life from Kenedy through the politics of the 1990s. We embarked on the research and preparations for the interviews during 1993, and began the actual taping sessions with Frances Goff in the fall of 1993. These sessions continued into the winter of 1994 when Frances's health began to falter, and the project concluded in August 1994 with one final interview a month before her death.

In the early stages of the interviews, it seemed possible that the transcript might become the basis for Frances Goff's memoirs, and several chapters were drafted in that form. It soon developed, however, that Frances would not be capable of completing a book in that way; and her death in September 1994 made the idea moot. The process of researching Frances's life and the interviews that we had done with her friends and colleagues convinced us that Frances Goff deserved a biographical treatment. The book that follows is our effort to provide an analytical narrative that illuminates the three careers that Frances Goff pursued: Texas politics, her ties with M. D. Anderson Hospital, and her involvement with the Bluebonnet Girls State program for four decades.

Although she had been an influential figure in the public life of Texas since the early 1940s, Frances Goff was largely unknown to the general public when she died. She had not sought the spotlight, and she realized that she could be more influential if she did not seek direct credit for all that she had done. Many people on the inside of the Texas political scene knew of her role in the state, and there were sporadic newspaper stories that touched on aspects of her career. This book is the first full examination of the life and times of an extraordinary person whose impact on the history of women in Texas deserves to be chronicled.

Frances Goff pursued three public careers. From the late 1930s until the end of her life, she played a role in state politics, first as an aide and supporter to such conservative Democratic figures as Coke Stevenson and Allan Shivers. During the 1950s she shifted her allegiance to the Republican party and supported the gubernatorial ambitions of Jack Cox from the end of that decade into the early 1960s. Goff also encouraged the political career of George Bush and other Republicans in Houston. In the late 1980s and into the early 1990s, Frances Goff became a close political adviser of Ann Richards, a commitment that she maintained until her death.

In her employment in state government, Frances Goff observed the development of Texas politics during the period of conservative Democratic ascendancy. Her work as secretary to various House and Senate committees in the 1940s, as well as her stint as budget director after World War II, made her a key player in the policies of the Beauford Jester and Allan Shivers administrations. Her activities provide new insights into the motivations and tactics of state leaders during that era.

A second career began for her when R. Lee Clark convinced her in 1951 to join him at the M. D. Anderson Cancer Hospital in Houston. Goff's involvement with special projects for the hospital, especially building construction and public events, allowed her to trace the evolution of Anderson into one of the great cancer treatment facilities in the world. The institutional and legislative history of M. D. Anderson was her individual preserve, and her memories of how the hospital grew provide a unique perspective on one of the major health institutions in Texas and the United States.

Closest to Frances Goff's heart was her third career as director of the Bluebonnet Girls State Program for the American Legion Auxiliary from 1951 until the summer of 1994. She poured her prodigious energies into making this citizenship education program a model for the entire country. In the process, she affected the lives of more than 20,000 young women in Texas. Historians have begun to recognize the importance of voluntary associations as significant forces in the lives of American women. Because of the American Legion Auxiliary's political conservatism, its programs to foster citizenship training have not received much attention from scholars.

In the case of Frances Goff, her work with the Citizens of Bluebonnet Girls State transcended ideological stereotypes. She wanted to instill in the women who came to the annual sessions the same love of politics that she had felt when she first came to Austin to work in the legislature. Goff resolved to make the Girls State sessions more than an evocation of patriotic feeling, although that was always a large element in what she did. Instead, she endeavored to provide realistic training in actual issues and governmental procedures. Moreover, she used her connections in state government to obtain the most prestigious speakers for the Girls State sessions. Her ability to operate as an equal in the male world of Texas politics told the Citizens that they might aspire to the same kind of influence and eventual power. Many of them followed her example, and Ann Richards in 1990 reached the pinnacle of Texas government.

The women who knew Frances Goff at Girls State attest that she was a shaping influence in their lives. An individual who guided several generations of Texas women toward public service and a lifelong involvement in politics deserves to have her career charted and her impact measured. This book will not exhaust the life of Frances Goff as a subject of historical inquiry. It does open up her three careers for careful scrutiny and assessment. At the same time, this narrative endeavors to recapture the human qualities that made Frances Goff such a special individual for so many people.

One of the most valuable contributions of women's studies has been to instruct historians that they should look for the role of women beyond the customary public spheres of elective office and political campaigns. Yet often the assumption has been that women best fulfill their obligations to society when they champion feminist causes or advance social agendas on the left of the political spectrum. Frances Goff's life illustrates the strengths and weaknesses of such a position. In her work for state government, M. D. Anderson, and Bluebonnet Girls State, she exemplified the kind of woman who made male-dominated institutions function and who used her connections with men to advance the interests of females. At the same time, she demonstrated that a woman could be conservative and, for much of her life, a Republican, and yet serve to raise the political consciousness and involvement of thousands of Texas women without insisting that they endorse her views or follow her lead. Frances Goff was a complicated individual, and this examination of her life seeks to do justice to the full range of her ideas and significant influence on Texas women in the twentieth century.

The title of this book emerged as we struggled with the problem of capturing in a single phrase or label all of the many ways in which Frances Goff played a role in recent Texas history. One underlying theme emerged. Goff had a passionate belief that an individual who benefited from a Texas education and the bounty of her native state had a duty to repay her fellow citizens by remaining in Texas. When former Citizens of Girls State asked her whether they should take professional opportunities outside of Texas, she encouraged them not to leave. This dedication to Texas expressed itself in the Girls State program when Goff led the Citizens in singing one of the many patriotic anthems that she loved so much. Since *Texas, Our Texas* was one of her special favorites, it seemed to us that a title embodying her affection for the state and its people best reflected the society and values to which Frances Goff had committed her life.[1]

Many people helped to make this book a reality. Anne Hodges Morgan first had the idea for an oral history about Frances Goff's life, and the energy, enthusiasm, and commitment that Anne Morgan infused into the project was indispensable at every stage of the research and writing. Her comments on draft chapters were always insightful and constructive. Rubyrae Phillips shared original source materials, commented on chapters, and gave unsparingly of her ideas and insights about Frances Goff and her career. Connie Bridges, the successor to Frances Goff at Bluebonnet Girls State, provided a thoughtful interview about Frances, facilitated the acquisition of the records of the Bluebonnet Girls State program for the University of Texas at Austin, and shared her infectious enthusiasm for the book with us. Judge Bea Ann Smith generously helped to get the project underway and was a source of many useful leads about Frances Goff's career. Gov. Ann Richards took time from her busy schedule to provide an interview about her friendship with Frances Goff and to promote the aims and purposes of the project.

Former Citizens of Girls State were most thoughtful in their willingness to share their memories and personal records. We are grateful to Ginger Allen, Casey Coffman, Ann Doan, Elaine Ginsburg, Marsha Grissom, Myra Hester, Maryana Iskander, Billee Lee, Jane Malaise, Patricia Mathis, Nancy Ohlendorf, Dale Simons, Mary Ellen Trahan, Arliss Treybig, and Teresa Zunker.

Friends of Frances Goff were also kind with their readiness to provide interviews. The late Senator James E. Taylor gave his recollections in 1993, and Ruth Wilson shared her memories of Frances in 1995. Michell Kraft played an important role in the early stages of the project.

---

[1] The names of women active in the American Legion Auxiliary are given as they described themselves at the time. For the Citizens of the Bluebonnet Girls State program, they are referred to by their full names at the first reference to them and then by the names they were known by at the time of their participation in the group's activities.

Frances Goff had hundreds, perhaps thousands, of friends and associates from her work with Bluebonnet Girls State, M. D. Anderson Hospital, and her years in politics. We are aware that not all of these people are mentioned in the narrative that follows. Doing full justice to all the ramifications of Goff's life would have demanded a book of far greater size than this one. We recognize in advance that numerous episodes and aspects of Frances's life will remain to be examined. We regard this book as an initial exploration of her fascinating life, and we hope that other biographers and historians will look into her contributions to Bluebonnet Girls State and M. D. Anderson in even greater detail. Our goal has been to bring the basic outline of Goff's role in the history of Texas to light so that her place in the modern development of the state can be understood. If anyone believes that more needs to be told about Goff's life and times, we urge them to write about their experiences with her as fully as possible.

The Goff Project could not have been funded without the support of President Robert Berdahl and former Vice President and Dean of the Graduate School William S. Livingston of the University of Texas at Austin. Bonnie Montgomery of the Department of History helped us with the day-to-day operations of the project with her customary efficiency and patience. We are also indebted to the M. D. Anderson Foundation and the Powell Foundation for financial assistance. Support from the Littlefield Fund for Southern History at the University of Texas at Austin facilitated final publication. We are grateful to Harold Billings for help with the Littlefield Fund's endorsement. Byron Hulsey did research in England about Frances Goff's family, and then provided indispensable assistance in organizing the Goff Papers when they came to the University of Texas. Jennifer Thornburrow contributed timely research in the A. M. Aikin Papers. Christie Bourgeois answered key questions about the Goff-Richards friendship in a timely fashion and with good cheer. The staffs at the County Clerk's Office and District Clerk's Office in the Karnes County Courthouse, the District Clerk's Office in the Bexar County Courthouse, and the Kenedy Public Library made a quick research trip most productive. Linda Fischer Luna at the Perry-Castañeda Library, University of Texas at Austin, did valiant labor in locating the microfilm editions of the Kenedy and Seguin newspapers. The staff of the Texas State Archives guided us through the Allan Shivers Papers with great skill.

The staff of the Center for American History at the University of Texas at Austin helped us acquire the Goff Papers and conduct this project in more ways than a single paragraph can acknowledge. We owe thanks to Don

Carleton and Kate Adams for their support and encouragement, and to William Richter, Ralph Elder, Deborah Bloys, Alison Beck, Trudy Croes, Andy Damico, Sara Clark, Ned Brierley, and Stefanie Wittenbach for their assistance with processing, researching, and photocopying from the Goff Papers and other collections.

Ron Tyler, George Ward, Janice Pinney, and William Bishel of the Texas State Historical Association provided superb editorial and production assistance with the publication of this book. The participants in Nancy Beck Young's seminar, Women and Texas Politics, provided valuable insight during the last stages of production. We offer our thanks to Jennifer Bretzel, Tesa Golden, Ahmad Hayes, Bonnie Martin, and Chauncey Taylor.

We are indebted to Jeff Rasco for his willingness to donate the Goff Papers to The University of Texas at Austin and for his hospitality and assistance during research trips in Houston, and to the members of his family for their support of this work about Frances Goff.

Karen Gould and Mark Young supported us during three years of research and writing about Frances Goff with prompt assistance, patience about the time it took from other duties, and with the shared conviction that the story of Frances Goff needed to be told.

Chapter 1

The Girl from Sixshooter Junction

It was her exciting introduction to the world of Texas politics. Frances Elizabeth Goff was only twelve years old during the summer of 1928 in the small East Texas town of Center where she lived with her mother, Grace Goff Stripling, and her stepfather, G. G. "Grad" Stripling, in a big house near the family drugstore. Frances was a mature girl for her age. She played softball and shared her mother's zest for poker and mah jongg. Yet her restless energy and quick mind sought more excitement and adventure. As her elders talked about the turbulent political scene in Texas during that presidential election year, Frances absorbed the local gossip about wets versus drys, the chances of the Democrats in the presidential contest, and who would be running for offices from sheriff to Congress.

A local attorney named S. H. "Spot" Sanders had an office across the street from the Stripling drugstore. He made it a habit to drop over and visit with Grace each day. In the spring of 1928, Sanders announced that he intended to challenge the renomination of the incumbent Congressman for the Second District, John C. Box, in the Democratic primary that July. Box was concluding his fourth term in 1928. His district sprawled across fourteen East Texas counties, and he experienced little trouble holding his seat during the earlier part of the decade. Undaunted, Sanders proclaimed his candidacy, and then, to her surprise, asked Frances if she would serve as his "Junior Campaign Manager." She agreed, and in the weeks that followed she joined the candidate's son Weldon in the back of the family roadster. Perched on the rickety rumble seat, she rattled down the red dirt roads of East Texas in search of votes.

In the end, Sanders lost to Box, but Frances Goff had gained a lifelong devotion to politics. She followed closely the events at the Democratic National Convention in Houston that nominated Al Smith for president

1

against the Republican Herbert Hoover. From the exposure that she received that summer to the end of her days, Frances Goff never got enough of Texas politics and those who practiced it.

She was born in Kenedy, Texas, on July 16, 1916, the only child of Alfred T. Goff and Grace Ingram Goff. In many ways, the difficult family history and background of the young Frances Goff provided an excellent preparation for the career in government and public service that she pursued until her death in 1994. At the time, however, childhood and adolescence was a period of family pain, tragedy, and dislocation. A broken home and the premature death of her mother dominated her early life.

The Goff side of Frances's family came to Kenedy a generation before her birth. Her grandfather, Percy Robert Goff, was born in Bedford, England, at 23 Adelaide Square on November 14, 1867. His father, Thomas Goff, was a grocer's assistant and his mother was Mary Clarabutt Goff. Percy had one other brother and two sisters. Family legend later had it that Percy's brother became the Lord Mayor of Peterborough, but official records do not list any Goff as holding that office.

England during the 1880s held few attractions for the young and energetic Percy Goff. He emigrated to the United States toward the end of the decade. Before he departed, his brother gave him a twenty-pound bank note to use in case of an emergency. Percy never had to spend the money, which would have been worth about a thousand dollars in modern currency. Frances Goff kept the note all of her life as one of her treasured possessions. When he arrived in New York City, Percy decided to board a train and travel across the United States until he found the economic opportunity that had brought him across the Atlantic.

He descended from the train for good at Seguin, Texas. At the time he arrived, Seguin was a flourishing community of twenty-three hundred people, located on the Guadalupe River about sixty miles southwest of the state capitol at Austin. Frances regarded it as ironic that the place her grandfather chose to live would become after 1970 the site for the annual programs of the Bluebonnet Girls State at Texas Lutheran College.

Railroads got into Percy Goff's blood. He went to work for the San Antonio and Aransas Pass Railroad, known to all in the area as the "SAP." Shortly thereafter the railroad transferred Percy to Yorktown, home of a large German settlement. There Percy met Ida Mary Reidle, the daughter of German immigrants. She was eighteen when she and Percy decided to be married in early 1890.

Percy and Ida Mary Goff family, ca. 1912. Top row, left to right: W. L "Bill" Goff, A. T. "Red" Goff, R. W. Goff. Seated, left to right: Blossom Goff, Mrs. Percy R. Goff Sr., Percy R. Goff Sr., Percy R. Goff Jr. *CN 08986. Courtesy Frances Goff Papers, Center for American History, University of Texas at Austin.*

A railroad accident changed the course of Percy Goff's life. After being hurt in Yorktown, he spent several months in the Santa Rosa Hospital in San Antonio. The delayed marriage ceremony took place on June 1, 1890, with Percy on crutches. His active career with the railroad was over, and he looked for some other way to make a living.

Like many small entrepreneurs in the 1890s, Percy Goff turned to serving the travelers that the railroads brought to the South Central Texas area. He and Ida Mary operated a rooming house in Yoakum where the SAP road had its repair shops. Several years later, when the railroad opened a roundhouse in Kenedy in Karnes County, the Goffs moved there. Kenedy had only 200 residents in 1896 when the village was ten years old. Named after Mifflin Kenedy, one of the builders of the railroad, the community had ambitions to grow.

During the next decade and a half Percy Goff prospered, though at some cost to his marriage. In 1909, he and Ida Mary were contemplating a divorce. Legal records in Karnes County show that their community property totaled more than $10,000, including eleven head of cattle, a wagon, and twenty-six bales of cotton. They also owned the furnishings and equipment of the Lane Hotel in Yoakum.

The couple reconciled, however, and by 1912 they had opened the Goff Hotel in Kenedy, a two-story structure that stood on one of the town's principal streets. During the middle of the decade, Percy Goff was an influential citizen of Kenedy. In 1914, he was the secretary of the Kenedy Commercial Club, and a few years later he became the town's mayor. His granddaughter recalled that he looked a little like Franklin D. Roosevelt and had lost any trace of an English accent. Her grandfather was the first businessman-politician that Frances Goff knew, and he became a model for the others that followed.

The Goff family grew during these years. There were five children in all, four boys and one girl. The second son in the Goff clan was Alfred Thomas Goff, born in 1893. By the time that the Goff Hotel opened its doors, Alfred was nineteen. He had finished his education at Kenedy High School and was working for the railroad. He had red curly hair, was of medium height, and every one called him "Red" Goff. He won accolades from the railroad for his initiative in rounding up some cattle that had gotten loose in the streets of Kenedy.

In a small town, Alfred Goff must have been aware of an attractive teenage girl who was already a favorite in the community for what the Kenedy *Advance* on November 23, 1923, called "her genial disposition and happy mannerisms." Grace Ingram had been born on February 12, 1896, in East Texas. Her parents had first met in Rusk, Texas, where her father, William Henry Ingram, was a doctor. Her mother, Hazel Ingram, experienced personal tragedies during the early years of her marriage. As Francis later told the story, her grandfather was preparing to leave on his medical rounds and his wife left one of their children "alone in a highchair in front of the fireplace." Hazel returned to find that the infant had fallen out of the chair, into the fireplace, and had perished before she could return.

Grace's father died of pneumonia in 1902 when he was just thirty-six, leaving his widow with a young son and daughter. Mrs. Ingram and her entire family moved to Kenedy around 1908. Grace grew up into an attractive, gregarious woman whose charm became fabled in the area. She was salutatorian of her graduating class at Kenedy High School in May 1912, and she told the

Grace Ingram, age eighteen. *CN 08959. Courtesy Frances Goff Papers, Center for American History, University of Texas at Austin.*

audience at the commencement ceremonies: "We know it is our duty to go forth into the world if we should make *the* 'success' which we all wish." She stressed the significant role of "character" in achieving success, and added, in words that would later shape her daughter's attitudes, "you cannot make friends by attempting to destroy the character of others."

Grace had dark, ash-blonde curly hair and a flair for the card and board games that were played constantly in the wide-open community of Kenedy. Known as "Six-Shooter Junction" for its violent ways, Kenedy was a town where gambling, saloons, and a relaxed night life flourished. How much young Grace moved in those circles before her marriage is not clear.

By late 1915, however, she and Alfred Goff had decided to get married. The Episcopal wedding took place at the Ingram home on October 12, 1915, before 100 guests. The Goffs honeymooned in San Antonio, Austin, and elsewhere with their friends Ruth Butler and Hollis Lee who had been married two days after the Goff nuptials. The local contributor for the San Antonio *Express*, reporting on October 17, 1915, said of Grace's wedding that "the display of presents was beautiful and elaborate."

The first year of the marriage seems to have been happy enough. Grace Goff was pregnant within a few months of the wedding. Frances Goff arrived in July 1916. In the little baby book that Grace kept and which her daughter preserved, she recorded Frances Goff's first laugh on October 25, 1916. Grace "rubbed her nose on her stomach and Miss Frances laughed. It caused such a laugh Grandmother Ingram had to come in to see what the fun was."

The birth of a daughter may have been more than Alfred Goff was ready for. In any case, by 1917 Alfred had begun treating Grace in a way that, as she later told a Texas court, represented "unkind, harsh conduct toward her." They quarreled often and Alfred cursed at his wife frequently. There may have been tensions because the couple lived with Grace's mother, who provided money for the newlyweds.

The split occurred in June 1918 when Alfred "in an angry and threatening manner struck [Grace] with his fist." The Goffs separated and Grace soon initiated divorce proceedings. Alfred moved out of Kenedy. The divorce case started in Karnes County, but the estranged husband and wife agreed to have the proceedings heard in San Antonio. The Bexar County judge ruled that a divorce should be granted. Grace was given custody of Frances and Alfred received generous visitation privileges. The court also decided that if Grace remarried then her mother would have custody of young Frances Goff.

Information about the background of the divorce has faded away after nearly eight decades. Frances said that her mother never talked about her

Grace Goff in 1925. *CN 08985. Courtesy Frances Goff Papers, Center for American History, University of Texas at Austin.*

marriage and refused to say a bad word about her former husband. When Frances knew her father later in her life, she found him to be a man with a jealous streak and a volatile temper. Whether he was jealous of Grace, or thought her too friendly with other men in Kenedy, cannot now be determined. For Frances Goff at the age of two, a separation of her parents must

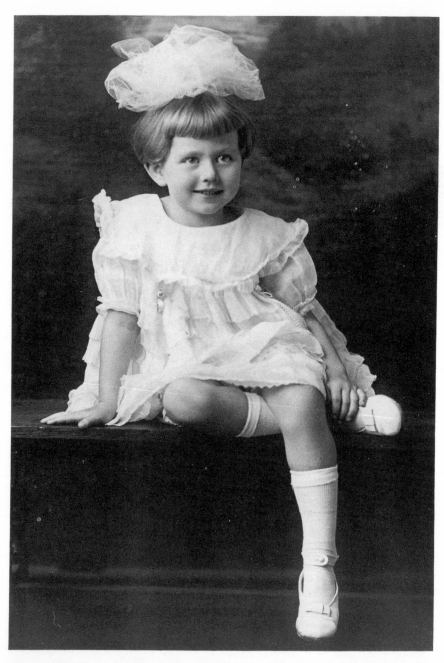

Frances Goff around age five. *CN 08990. Courtesy Frances Goff Papers, Center for American History, University of Texas at Austin.*

have been an event that she could not understand. Their divorce a year later compounded the shock, especially at a time and in a community where broken marriages were not the rule.

Following her divorce, Grace Goff and Frances remained in Kenedy for four years. The Kenedy *Advance* affords some glimpses of "little Miss Frances Goff." In March 1920, she visited her father who was working as a railroad cashier in Alice, Texas. A few months later, she was a guest at the fifth birthday party of Ernestine Bain. Meanwhile, Grace led an active social life. The *Advance* noted her frequent attendance at the Friday Social Club, the Bridge Club, and the 500 Club. She and Frances were at the Kenedy All Nite Club in May 1923 where "dancing was enjoyed until a late hour," according to a news item of May 3, 1923.

As for Alfred Goff, he wandered in and out of his daughter's early childhood. In April 1920 he became a cashier at Corpus Christi, and three years later was employed by the National Compress Company in Waxahachie. He had married a Kenedy woman named Elizabeth Nave who was a close friend of Grace Goff. These fleeting occasions left Frances with no clear memories of her father, and her closeness to her mother grew.

Kenedy lived up to its violent reputation during the early years of Frances's life. She recalled how, in the months before her fifth birthday, she witnessed a murder near the Goff Hotel. The victim was Hollis Lee who, with his new bride, had accompanied the Goffs on their honeymoon trip in 1915. By 1920 Lee was supposedly having an affair with the wife of F. H. "Jabbie" Burrus. Frances was sitting in a car on May 22, 1921, when Burrus gunned down Lee. Although the prosecution summoned fifteen witnesses to the crime (Frances was not among them), it proved impossible to get a jury impaneled and the case was dismissed six years later.

During the spring of 1923, Grace Goff, her mother, "and little Miss Frances Goff" went back to East Texas to the town of Teneha for a month-long stay. There Grace either met or renewed a friendship with G. G. "Grad" Stripling, a druggist in Center, a World War I veteran, and a member of "an old East Texas family." They were married on November 26, 1923, in a small ceremony again at the Ingram home, this time with a Baptist minister officiating. The Striplings, and presumably Frances Goff, left "on the night train for Center where they will make their home," said the *Advance* of November 29.

The move to East Texas was not a happy one for Frances at the start. Accustomed to the more relaxed lifestyle of South Texas and to a certain degree of affluence that allowed her mother to shop for clothes in San Antonio stores, the seven-year-old girl initially did not fit in well with her rural playmates. When her mother dressed her in a red and blue dress for school, the children taunted her with the rhyme: "Red and Blue, tacky too! Red and blue, tacky too!" On some days, they pelted Frances with stones as she walked home. She told her mother that she did not want to return to school. Her mother also found the atmosphere of Center somewhat confining. In an undated letter to her mother, Grace complained: "I've read everything I can find around here—books and magazines. I have the car, but there's not any where much to go."

As the weeks and months passed, however, Frances and her mother found themselves more accepted at Center. Grace's affinity for card games proved infectious, and she and her daughter introduced mah jongg and bridge to a community that had not heard of these diversions before. As Frances told an interviewer in 1993, her mother "had a party almost every day because the people wanted to learn from her."

In grammar school, Frances played on the girls softball team. She was a natural athlete and was proficient at a number of sports. She pitched and was, as she remembered, "a pretty good hitter." Her softball career ended, however, when she hit her best friend, Avis Cook, in the forehead with a bat. The sport was never the same to her after that episode. As the years passed, Frances found the town more to her liking. She was called Frances Stripling in the Center Public Schools. In the fifth grade, on the report cards in her personal papers, she received mostly As with only two Bs in writing and grammar, and she was promoted to the sixth grade. Her performance in the seventh grade was more mixed, with a sprinkling of Bs and Cs. She finished elementary school in May 1929.

Amid all of her interest in politics and the demands of school, Frances remained close to her youthful mother. Her fondest personal memories were of the backyard of the house. Frances often climbed the large tree, and her mother would come out and join her in its branches. Other nights, she would pitch a tent in the yard, and they would spend the night there together, reading and talking. The surviving letters of young Frances Goff suggest a happy family in Center. Writing to her mother in May 1925, she said that "since you and Daddy have helped me in every way, I should like to make you happy. I have no carnation to send so I am writing this letter. It is too small to carry all my love for you, but I hope it will carry some."

Youth came to an end suddenly for Frances Goff in 1929 when her mother became ill and died from pneumonia on June 29. The crisis happened so quickly that Frances had almost no time to spend with her mother before she died. In the days before penicillin, there was little the doctors could do once

Frances Goff as a teenager. *CN 08991. Courtesy Frances Goff Papers, Center for American History, University of Texas at Austin.*

the disease became established. It was a moment of great grief to a girl on the brink of adolescence.

The ceremony reflected the shock of the small community of Center at Grace Stripling's death. Frances Goff kept the newspaper account of her mother's funeral that said "floral offerings were so numerous as to necessitate distributing over several cars in the long procession which wound slowly in the direction of Fairview Cemetery. Mrs. Stripling was among the most popular of Center's social set as well as being devoted to affairs of church and home." The story said that she had one daughter, Frances Stripling.

After the funeral, Frances accompanied her Goff grandparents back to Kenedy. She had not cut her hair during the period of her mother's illness, and she recalled in 1993 that it was "long and disheveled." Her grandmother took her to a beauty parlor for a haircut. When Frances awoke the next day, her hair had turned curly with distinctive ringlets. It remained that way for the rest of her life or, as she put it, "I have never been able to calm my hair down since." Her body reacted to the emotional loss in other ways. In letters to her maternal grandmother, she reported that she "had the tummy ache all day yesterday & this evening." One Sunday, as she prepared to go to Sunday School, she was unable to tie the strings on a dress "like mama could and I began to just squall. I do not know how I am going to live without her."

The practical issue of where teenage Frances was going to live confronted her family too. Her father had told her by telegram: "if you need anything wire your daddy," but it soon became clear that she could not stay with Alfred Goff and his second wife. During a discussion in Kenedy about whether they would take Frances home with them, she overheard Elizabeth Goff's irate question to Percy Goff: "You had to bring that brat back here with you, didn't you?" For Frances, her first thought was: "Where do you go from here?"

Staying with her stepfather was also not an option. Grad Stripling had taken his wife's death very hard. Since druggists were allowed to sell alcohol for medicinal purposes during Prohibition, "Strip" had been a popular man in Center. Apparently, he had begun sampling some of his own stock and had become a virtual alcoholic even before Grace died. Now in his distraught condition, he would not have been able to deal with custody of a teenage girl.

One of the letters that Frances Goff wrote to him has survived. In it, her characteristic voice and authority emerge for the first time. Her mother, she told Grad, was "in a better place than she was on earth. She worried so much and had so much trouble, and now she has no more trouble, sorrow or pain." She urged him to "please be the man you ought to be for my sake and others." At her Grandmother Goff's urging, she told him that her name was "Goff not Stripling" and that he should so address future letters to her.

In the early weeks after her mother's death, Frances wrote often of her desire to return to Center. "I long for all my friends in Center," she wrote to her grandmother. She complained that in Kenedy "I don't seem to be in the right place here. The girls my age don't give bridge parties and women smoke ain't that terrible and I want to go back to Center and live with you."

With her three grandparents living in Kenedy and Stripling unable to help her, Frances found that Kenedy was where she was going to reside for the immediate future. Although she missed her mother intensely, Frances came to enjoy her teenage years in Kenedy at the Goff Hotel. By the end of the 1920s, the Hotel was a lively focus of social activity in the small town. It had sixty rooms and some twenty employees. The place filled up during the week, and then emptied out on weekends as the professional travelers returned to their homes. As Frances remembered it, "the fun never stopped" from Monday through Friday. There was a poker game every night, and a slot machine operated in a corner. In the hotel lobby, the guests played bridge, Forty-Two, and shoot-the-moon. Holidays were a rollicking time with the spiked eggnog flowing from ten-gallon containers in the hotel kitchen. Prohibition touched Kenedy lightly, and bootlegging occurred throughout Karnes County.

Grandfather Percy insisted that Frances learn to drink at home rather than at a speakeasy. When the family gathered on Saturday nights for his "dutch lunch," Percy made the beer himself. Frances would join him at his home, and sit on the floor with beer bottles all around her. Her task was to place a teaspoonful of sugar in each bottle while Percy would siphon the beer behind her. They would spend the day doing it, and she relished the times when he would call her and say: "It is time for us to bottle again." Frances Goff grew up in that hard-drinking era and became accustomed to alcohol as part of the social world in which she lived. Sometime during her teenage years, she also became a smoker, a habit that stayed with her until late in her life.

Residing in the Goff Hotel turned out to be the ideal preparation and fore-runner of the political world that Frances Goff entered a decade later. She gained an exposure to the male culture of the time as she saw and then participated in the nonstop drinking, gambling, and partying at the hotel. She developed skills for surviving and rising in the world of small-town Texas politics that other young women of her generation from traditional backgrounds rarely saw. At the same time, her unconventional childhood experience and the memories of her mother's difficult marriages meant that she did not regard marriage and childrearing as inevitable choices for her.

The Great Depression only grazed Kenedy. An oil boom, a growing demand for the onions raised in the area, and the cotton buyers kept the Goff Hotel filled. Frances loved to wander through the rooms where the traveling salesmen displayed their wares for people to view. When Franklin D. Roosevelt declared a bank holiday in March 1933, the Goffs were the only people with cash in the town, and the citizens used the hotel as their bank until the financial crisis ebbed.

Friends of Frances Goff recalled that growing up in the hotel molded her character as a leader and politician. Getting to know the individuals who passed through the Goff Hotel lobby gave her a superb introduction to a rising generation of state political leaders. Among the frequent guests was a lawyer from Junction in Kimble County, Coke Stevenson, whom Frances would know later when he was speaker of the Texas House, lieutenant governor, and governor.

Another friendship that Frances had during the Kenedy years proved significant for her later professional life. A local doctor started a hospital in Kenedy, and then recruited a surgeon for the staff. The physician was named John W. Worsham, and he brought his new wife, Dorothy Clark Worsham, to Kenedy with him. The couple lived at the Goff Hotel where Frances got to know them well. Dorothy Clark's brother was Randolph Lee Clark, the future director of M. D. Anderson Hospital in Houston and Frances's boss there.

One person who did not impress Frances Goff at this time was the young Lyndon Johnson. They had friends in common in the Sam Fore family of nearby Floresville. Frances also knew John Connally's sister when the two young women dated the same boy. The Fores were eager for Frances to meet Johnson because of their mutual interest in politics. Johnson was twenty-four in 1932, and working for Congressman Richard Kleberg. Surely Frances and Lyndon would hit it off. They did not, and Frances developed a dislike for Johnson in the years that followed.

Frances Goff attended Kenedy High School with the class of 1933. She played on the tennis team and acted in theatrical productions. When the senior class put on "The Touchdown" in April 1933, Frances took the role of Rena Maynard. The reporter for the Kenedy *Advance* described her on April 6 as "refined, pretty, and daintily coquettish" in the part. In a poem written for her graduation, a classmate said of her: "Frances Goff, whose songs you hear, is seldom without her good old cheer."

In her last year of high school, Frances received a series of love letters from a student at Texas A&M University, Robert Barnett. He wrote her continuously, if irregularly, during the autumn. They had some photographs taken in one of the booths that produced several images for a dime or a quarter. Her letters to him have not survived, but his anxious remarks indicate that Barnett did not monopolize her social life. He complained when she attended dances

Frances Goff and Robert Barnett. *CN 08949. Courtesy Frances Goff Papers, Center for American History, University of Texas at Austin.*

without him, but also cautioned her: "don't get too serious—you remember we are both school kids." In a subsequent letter, he added: "we can be *real good friends* and go together lots & have lots of fun." After December 1932 the letters ended.

The grades that Frances achieved in her senior year were only average, but her brisk social life continued. During June 1933, at the invitation of the

Chapter 2

Austin and the World of Texas Politics

On September 27, 1937, Frances Goff arrived at the Texas state capitol. The first thing that she did when she settled down to work in the legislature was to read the lengthy Texas Constitution of 1876 all the way through. Her mastery of the intricacies of state government grew as she observed the floor proceedings and the maneuvers in the cloakrooms. She was, as she later put it, an inveterate "people watcher," and she devoted hours to tracking the politicians in action. The pace of the legislative process enthralled her. Meanwhile, Helmuth Schuenemann gave Goff great leeway. He was patient with her and allowed her to move around and get to know other members.

Although she loved the legislature from the outset, her transition to state government was not a smooth process. The 1937 session was soon over, however, and Frances returned to Kenedy to help her grandparents run the Goff Hotel. Opportunity for financial advancement then beckoned when the Commercial Credit Company asked her to go to Corpus Christi as a secretary to an office manager. She spent six months on the job before her grandparents, whose marital difficulties had returned, told her that they were retiring from the hotel business. In June 1938, she moved back to Kenedy where she remained for the rest of the year.

In January 1939, the legislature reconvened for its regular session, and Frances Goff once again joined Helmuth Schuenemann in the House of Representatives. Her interrupted political education now resumed. Conditions for legislative secretaries were primitive by modern standards. Members did not have separate offices. Instead, the secretaries sat in the rear of the House chamber, along a corridor. Each secretary had a small table, ten or twelve inches by fourteen inches on which their typewriters rested. When

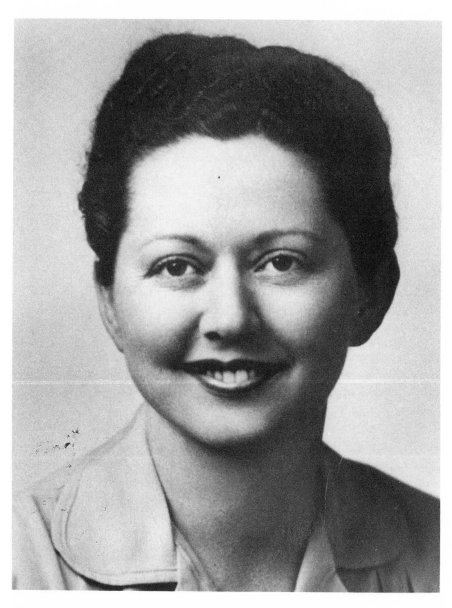

Frances enters the legislature, 1937. *CN 08969. Courtesy Frances Goff Papers, Center for American History, University of Texas at Austin.*

Goff took dictation from Schuenemann, she had to go down into the House and sit on the floor next to his desk. The files were kept in boxes beneath his desk. Deliberations of the House continued while she worked. She scribbled dictation as the debates swirled around her.

In many respects, the Texas legislature and the state capitol resembled a kind of political hotel, much like what Frances Goff had grown up with in Kenedy. It had the same openness to the public throughout the day with constituents, lobbyists, legislators, and aides coming and going on their many errands. The same rhythms of meals, meetings, and recreation governed the schedule of those involved. To pass the time, members played cards, exchanged gossip, and worked out social occasions much as they would have done in a hotel lobby anywhere in the state. It was a network of "good ol' boys" into which Frances Goff's background enabled her to blend easily. The lawmakers recognized her competence and discretion, and admitted her to the laid-back world that ran state politics.

Under the close conditions of the House, members and their secretaries got to know the people who sat near them. Schuenemann became a close friend of James "Jim" Taylor of Kerens, a future boss of Frances Goff's in the Texas Senate. She knew other members, and they visited the local Mexican restaurants together. She watched the skilled debaters, such as G. C. Morris of Somerville, and noted how they swayed the House at key moments. She learned to deal with the lobbyists when they sought inside information from her. It was an exciting political apprenticeship for her.

She put the gambling skills that she had learned at the Goff Hotel to work. Several House members spent hours playing dominoes. Among the participants were Homer Thornberry, a future Congressman and federal judge, and Homer Leonard, a future Speaker of the House. Goff was able to keep score for a domino game, and she sat in the appropriations committee chambers recording who won and lost. The representatives talked candidly in front of her because they knew that she would preserve their confidences.

Frances remembered the Texas legislature as a small, friendly community. She lived for a time at the Williams Hotel on Eleventh Street, and then moved into a house near the capitol with a basement apartment that she shared with a friend named Martha Long. They dined at Mrs. Elliott's boarding house where meals cost thirty-five cents per day. Occasionally, they ate out at the Blue Bird Cafe or other boarding houses. Around the table, they might see the governor or attorney general passing their plates like everyone else. Men and women went to football games, danced in the evenings, and

Sen. Jim Taylor. *CN 08941. Courtesy Frances Goff Papers, Center for American History, University of Texas at Austin.*

partied in the Hill Country and out on the Highland Lakes that were being built in those years.

The city of Austin had about 67,000 residents in the late 1930s, and the University of Texas at Austin enrolled some 7,000 students. Most of Austin's population lived within a few miles of the state capitol that dominated the skyline. Frances Goff soon became part of a subculture of women who worked in the legislature or the state government. Although Texas politics was a man's world, the women kept the machinery operating, and a kind of camaraderie existed among those who were in Austin.

The Depression still affected the state's economy, but life in Austin was pleasant and inexpensive. Frances Goff could walk to work or take a streetcar. When she got to the capitol that was not yet air conditioned, she would find animals that had come in the open windows during the night. The rats, foxes, and possums scattered as the employees returned in the morning.

Gov. W. Lee "Pappy" O'Daniel. *CN 08129. Courtesy Jimmie A. Dodd Photograph Collection, Center for American History, University of Texas at Austin.*

While she worked in the House during 1939, Frances Goff had a chance to observe the emergence of a new force in state politics. A year earlier, Wilbert Lee "Pappy" O'Daniel, a flour salesman from Fort Worth, became Governor. A well-known radio personality who broadcast statewide every day at 12:30 P.M., he offered the music of country swing artist Bob Wills and a band called the Lightcrust Doughboys. He marketed Hillbilly Flour with infectious songs:

> Hillbilly music on the air
> Hillbilly flour everywhere
> It tickles your feet—It tickles your tongue
> Wherever you go, its praises are sung.

Each program began with a woman's voice saying to O'Daniel: "Please pass the biscuits, Pappy."

Promising "less Johnson grass and politicians, more smokestacks and businessmen," O'Daniel swept to victory in the 1938 Democratic primary. He won the governorship without a runoff in an election that left seasoned political observers groping for explanations. The arrival of O'Daniel in Austin, however, opened a turbulent era of state politics, much of which Frances Goff witnessed in person. The Democratic Party split into rival factions with conservative governors in the ascendancy.

The first thing O'Daniel did was to propose a constitutional amendment to adopt a sales tax. The amendment would have kept taxes low on oil and natural gas while hitting consumers with levies on what they purchased. The idea aroused a storm of opposition, led by a group of lawmakers that dubbed themselves "The Immortal 56." Among the leaders of the anti-O'Daniel forces was Margaret Harris Amsler, a first-term representative from Waco, with whom Frances became friendly. Amsler's father had been dean of the Baylor Law School, and she later became the first female law professor in Texas at Baylor. In an election surprise in 1938, she defeated seven male opponents. She put her career on the line to stop the tax amendment. When it came for a vote, time after time Amsler and the other fifty-five dissenting members pushed their voting buttons in a solid bloc. As a result, the amendment never went to the voters for their approval. Frances noted, however, that Amsler was defeated in her 1940 race for reelection. Nonetheless, Goff had begun making contacts among the women in Texas politics that would help form the basis for her networks when she operated the Bluebonnet Girls State program for the American Legion Auxiliary from 1952 to 1994.

After the 1939 session ended, Frances Goff accepted an offer from an attorney in San Antonio named Fred Felty to work as his secretary. He had been in the legislature during Frances's stay there, and he recognized her abilities. Felty and his partner John Peace were powerful operators in local politics in Bexar County, and the opportunity added to Frances's store of good political friends. John Peace would become chairman of the Board of Regents of the University of Texas at Austin during the 1970s, and a valuable ally when Frances worked at M. D. Anderson Hospital.

During the late spring of 1940, Felty received a phone call from William "Bill" Lawson, then a close aide to Governor O'Daniel. Frances Goff had known Lawson in Center. He asked whether Goff could come to Austin to work for O'Daniel. The governor's relations with the press were rocky, and O'Daniel needed someone who could communicate with the reporters.

Bill McGill, ca. 1923. *CN 08906. From* Cactus, *1923. Courtesy Center for American History, University of Texas at Austin.*

O'Daniel had been nominated for a second term in 1940, and was again assured of election. However, his stock with the legislature was low. If he had ambitions to run for the U.S. Senate in the future, he needed a successful legislative program in 1941. Since Frances Goff already knew so many people in the press corps, she seemed an ideal choice to mend O'Daniel's fences with the newsmen and women. She saved an article from the Kenedy *Advance* that said she was "one of Kenedy's fine young women who is making a good record in her chosen line, and her many friends here will rejoice in her advancement."

Before Frances Goff left for Austin, her grandmother cautioned her about serving with the mercurial O'Daniel. "You're going up there to work for somebody that you don't really respect." That statement summarized Goff's mixed feelings about the governor. Nonetheless, since Fred Felty had ambitions to be O'Daniel's secretary of state, she believed that a good performance on her part might help him gain the position he wanted. "I'm sort of between a rock and a hard place right now," she told her grandmother.

Frances Goff worked for Pappy O'Daniel for only nine months from the spring of 1940 through the early weeks of 1941, but she was very much involved in the governor's activities. She developed several close friendships that proved significant for her in the years that followed. O'Daniel's personal secretary was Margaret McDuffie, and she and Frances later shared a house in Austin for several years. Frances remembered McDuffie as the finest typist she ever knew. McDuffie had to be good because the demanding O'Daniel kept his secretaries busy accommodating to his swift changes of mood about speeches and statements. Both Frances and Margaret proved to be resilient and capable. Secretary of State Lawson told the Kenedy newspaper that Goff and McDuffie were his "right hand men" and said "he just doesn't know what he would do without them."

Another personal tie was to O'Daniel's aide, William "Bill" McGill. As a University of Texas student in the mid-1920s, McGill had founded the Texas Cowboys, a spirit and service organization, that later pledged such prominent Texans as Senator Lloyd Bentsen and heart surgeon Denton Cooley. McGill also devised the yearly Roundup celebration in the spring that evolved into one of the highpoints in the recurrent series of parties that marked campus life in the years between the world wars. McGill and McDuffie became fixtures in the offices of future governors, and their esteem for Frances Goff was one foundation of her future political influence.

Two other renewed acquaintances from this period did not turn out so well. She met Lyndon Johnson again and worked with him at Governor O'Daniel's request on ideas to increase airplane traffic in the state. Spending two weeks consecutively with Johnson confirmed Frances's low opinion of the young Congressman. "He was just too high and mighty, and everything had to be his way," was her 1993 verdict.

The other disappointment concerned Bill Lawson. Goff's acquaintance with him had led her to the governor's office. Yet once Goff was on the staff Lawson offended her with the personal advances that a subsequent generation would call sexual harassment. She was reluctant in the 1990s to talk about the specifics of what had occurred, but it was clear from what she did

Railroad Commissioner Jerry Sadler, 1940.*CN 08743. From Jerry Sadler (with James Neyland),* Politics, fat-cats & honey-money boys: the Mem-wars of Jerry Sadler *(Santa Monica, Calif.: Roundtable Publishers, 1984), frontispiece. Courtesy Center for American History, University of Texas at Austin.*

about the specifics of what had occurred, but it was clear from what she did say that he had made unwelcome overtures to her.

Goff did not take to Governor O'Daniel either. She believed that his wife Merle dominated his administration, and that the governor lacked the ability to anticipate the personal and political consequences of his actions. Since his standing with the Texas legislature was so poor, before the lawmakers reconvened in January 1941, O'Daniel decided to visit all the members at their homes. Goff was assigned the task of preparing a biographical resume on each of the legislators which the O'Daniels used when they embarked on their tour. The experience gave her an inside look at the legislature and added to her store of political experience. The tour received favorable press coverage, which aroused some resentment against her among the governor's inner circle. The talk was that she was too friendly with the capitol reporters.

Her job put her in the governor's reception room of the capitol where visitors came to see O'Daniel. She was, according to her hometown newspaper, O'Daniel's "first line of defense." She greeted visitors "with a kindly consideration that causes them to go away happy whether they get to see the Governor or not." Yet not all encounters were tranquil. One day Goff heard a strange snapping noise outside in the foyer. She went through the large doors and encountered a man cracking a bull whip. She immediately told him: "Stop that!"

The man looked at her and said: "Why?"

She replied: "Because this is the Governor's Reception Room, we have people in here, and you get out of here with that bullwhip."

In her haste, Frances Goff did not notice that the man with the whip was Railroad Commissioner Jerry Sadler. When she realized later who he was, she feared that she had offended a powerful state official. But as O'Daniel lurched from internal crisis to internal crisis, she did not have time to worry about her apparent political gaffe.

Christmas 1940 brought an event that symbolized in Frances Goff's mind the disorganization with which "Pappy" O'Daniel operated. The governor delivered radio broadcasts every Sunday morning, but he rarely informed his staff about what he planned to say. He typed his text out in advance himself, and did not hand it to Margaret McDuffie to prepare for radio delivery until the last minute. On this occasion, two weeks before Christmas, he went on the radio and described "how hundreds of drab and dreary homes can this Christmas be made into the most happy and cheerful homes in Texas." He announced a plan to have one thousand "little orphan boys and girls" from the State Homes in Waco and Corsicana distributed to private homes during

W. O. "Otey" Reed. *CN 08943. Courtesy Frances Goff Papers, Center for American History, University of Texas at Austin.*

what O'Daniel dubbed "Christmas Orphan Visiting Week."

O'Daniel revealed that he had not disclosed the scheme to anyone before announcing it, and the scheme was certainly news to Frances Goff, Bill McGill, and the staff. The governor departed from his prepared text and told his audience that if they wished to participate in the program they just had to "call Bill McGill and Frances Goff, and they'll take care of it." Frances Goff and McGill spent the two weeks before Christmas working with the Department of Public Safety to get the children placed into the homes they would be visiting, and then returning them to state institutions once the holidays were over. The flood of inquiries and the logistics of handling so many young children tested the patience and skill of the two gubernatorial aides. As Bill McGill put it to Goff at one especially trying moment: "If there's ever been chaos agitated with an eggbeater, this is it." The phrase reappeared in Goff's personal comments for years afterward.

On the surface, Frances Goff was a great success as O'Daniel's secretary. By this time, however, Frances Goff's standing with the press had aroused animosities within O'Daniel's circle. His aides bridled at stories like the one from the Kenedy paper, which Goff saved, that urged visitors to the capitol to meet her. "You'll enjoy a conversation with her equally as much as you would with the governor. Modest, affable, and kindly, Miss Goff is a credit to anyone's office force." In addition, William Lawson wanted to become secretary of state, and there was no need to conciliate Fred Felty by keeping Frances Goff in the governor's office. She knew none of this until the incoming chairman of the House appropriations committee, W. O. "Otey" Reed, invited her to dinner. "I really need to talk with you about something," he told her.

When they were at dinner, he asked her if she knew that "You're going to be fired on Monday."

Goff responded: "I wouldn't mind it, I really wouldn't mind it."

Reed asked her to become the chief clerk of the appropriations committee. His inquiries about her at O'Daniel's office brought him the news of her imminent firing. So she decided to leave the governor before she could be fired, and return once again to the House of Representatives. She was, said one press story, "too nice to newspapermen" to remain with O'Daniel's staff.

Looking back on her brief service with Pappy O'Daniel, Frances Goff decided that he should never have been governor of Texas. Compared to the other governors she worked with and knew, from Coke Stevenson to Ann Richards, O'Daniel seemed unqualified for the high position he held. She attributed his initial success to "the little sing-song bit that he did on radio," but believed that once he took office "he had no idea how a governor should act or what he should do."

When Frances Goff left the governor's office to work on the House appropriations committee in February 1941, the legislature was in the early stages of what would be its longest session in the state's history up to that time. Adding to the problems of the lawmakers was the death of U.S. Sen. Morris Sheppard on April 9. That set up a special senatorial election in which Gov.

W. Lee O'Daniel, Cong. Lyndon B. Johnson, and Cong. Martin Dies were among the twenty-nine candidates. The outcome of that contest directly affected Goff's political fortunes. When O'Daniel won a seat in the U.S. Senate, Lt. Gov. Coke Stevenson, by now a close friend of Frances Goff, succeeded him.

For the moment, she reveled in her new responsibilities in the House. The Speaker was Homer Leonard, one of her domino players. He and his allies in the leadership faced intense problems in finding money for state services. Prosperity was returning as the economy went on a war footing, but the state remained in tough financial straits. Hard decisions flowed toward Frances's boss on the appropriations committee, W. O. Reed.

Working with "Otey" Reed was much more pleasant for Frances Goff than her months with Pappy O'Daniel had been. Reed had served in the House since 1933 and was a self-taught attorney from Dallas. A small, slim man with a thin mustache and steel-framed glasses, he was intensely superstitious. The number thirteen was his charm, and he usually filed for reelection as close to Friday the thirteenth as he could. Reed sometimes proved temperamental, but Goff found that she could work with him on a professional basis.

Among the issues that the legislature faced in the winter of 1941 was one that had a profound effect on Frances Goff's life. On February 5, Rep. Arthur Cato of Weatherford introduced House Bill 268 to create "a State Cancer Hospital for the treatment of cancer and allied diseases." The proposed law would have set up a three-member Cancer Commission, authorized the appointment of an administrator and staff to operate the facility, and established an advisory board of nine private citizens. Cato asked that a million dollars be appropriated for the hospital.

Concern about cancer was intensifying as the 1940s began. Four hundred thousand Americans died each year from the disease, which was the second leading cause of death behind heart disease. Public pressure for federal action led Congress and the U.S. Public Health Service to create the National Cancer Institute in 1937. Cong. Maury Maverick of San Antonio was one of the leaders on Capitol Hill of the cancer crusade.

Within Texas, the Texas Medical Association and the Women's Field Army of the American Society for the Control of Cancer gathered support for a cancer hospital to treat indigent patients. During 1941, the momentum for a state-supported cancer hospital accelerated. The medical establishment wanted to have such a facility in place as soon as possible. Representative Cato's reasons were more personal. A pharmacist himself, he had seen several members of his family, including his parents, die from the disease.

31

Gov. Coke Stevenson, inscribed "To My Longtime Friend Frances with every good wish, Coke Stevenson." *CN 08953. Courtesy Frances Goff Papers, Center for American History, University of Texas at Austin.*

When the supporters of cancer research in Texas looked at the Cato bill, however, they identified several immediate drawbacks. The measure set up a separate cancer facility in competition with the other eleemosynary institutions that the state funded. As a result, in the future the cancer hospital would be jockeying for funds with the School for the Blind, the School for the Deaf, the Confederate Home, and other comparable facilities. During each two-year cycle of the legislature, the cancer treatment center would have to seek money from lawmakers, and its funding would never be secure or predictable.

This aspect of the Cato bill particularly worried the dean of the University of Texas Medical Branch at Galveston, Dr. John Spies. Although he was an M.D., Spies lacked support from Texas doctors. He had become a controversial figure in state politics because of a dispute with his faculty over his leadership of the school in 1941. The doctors in Galveston were already working behind the scenes with the governor and the board of regents to have him fired. One of Spies's projects was to have a cancer research center established in Texas. He intended to have the law for the cancer hospital put responsibility for the facility under the University of Texas Board of Regents, perhaps with himself as the first administrator of the institution.

As a result of Spies's efforts, the Cato bill underwent modifications in committee to achieve the goals that the medical establishment desired. Cato submitted an amended version that put the Texas State Cancer Hospital and the Division of Cancer Research within "the control and management" of the University of Texas. The university would have the authority to fix the location of the hospital and hire an administrator. The proposed law laid out the powers of the university and the hospital director in great detail. Cato tried to move the bill through quickly, but the House did not agree to a fast-track approach. Still, there was a clear majority for the measure, and it passed the House by a vote of 85 to 39 on May 29, 1941.

Frances Goff knew why the House had voted so strongly for the amended Cato bill. Her role as clerk of the appropriations committee gave her an excellent vantage point to see what had occurred. The lieutenant governor in 1941 was Coke Stevenson, whom she had known during her adolescence in Kenedy. Stevenson was fifty-three in 1941, and had served in the legislature since 1929. Four years after first coming to the capitol, he was elected Speaker of the House. His term proved so successful that in 1935 he was the first person ever reelected Speaker.

One of Stevenson's biggest political assets was his wife Faye. Frances Goff remembered her in 1993 as "a lovely, lovely lady who always had something good to say about everyone." When Coke was reelected Speaker in 1935, Faye Stevenson came to the door of the chamber with a bouquet of roses. She handed them out one by one to the eighty members who voted for her husband.

Stevenson left the House after refusing a third term, ran for lieutenant governor in 1938, won in a runoff, and took office in January 1939. He was elected to a second term in 1940. A few months later, Faye Stevenson was diagnosed with breast cancer. Everyone in the legislature knew of her fate. The Stevensons lived in the suite of the lieutenant governor in the capitol, and she was failing all during the winter and spring of 1941.

The Cato bill came before the appropriations committee on a cold winter night in 1941. Francis Goff heard a member of the House, Fred Red Harris, appeal to his colleagues to support the measure. A feisty Dallas lawmaker who earned his nickname as a high school football player, Fred Harris had his name legally changed to Fred Red. An intimate of the Stevensons, Harris enjoyed fighting both on the floor and in the cloakroom where he had several punching episodes. On this winter night, however, his purpose was humanitarian.

Harris moved for the adoption of the bill, and then observed: "There's a woman that we all love very much and respect, and she's across the rotunda in the Lieutenant Governor's suite dying of this disease, and we need to do something about it." He urged his colleagues to get the cancer hospital started. Ironically, Harris himself later died of cancer. With the example of Faye Stevenson before them and with the support of her friends in the legislature, the bill to create a cancer hospital proceeded to ultimate passage and received Governor O'Daniel's signature on June 30, 1941.

Faye Stevenson lived to see Coke become governor of Texas on August 2, 1941. O'Daniel had won the Senate race over Lyndon Johnson in a tight election that featured charges of fraud in the counting of the ballots. Stevenson's wife lingered on for five more months. Frances Goff attended her funeral in Junction in what she remembered as one of the coldest days of her life. The size of the crowd of mourners also stayed in her memory.

In the aftermath of his wife's death, Governor Stevenson became a very lonely man. To have people around him, he asked friends to visit him during the evenings. An enthusiastic dancer, Stevenson kept music playing constantly, and, Frances Goff recalled, "would jump up, pull me up to join him, and we would dance and dance and dance."

Frances Goff now shared an apartment with Margaret McDuffie who was also close to Stevenson. He invited the two women to spend weekends at his

Frances Goff between Martha Long and Nub Johnson or Bill Corry at Marshall Ford Dam, June 4, 1939. *CN 08944. Courtesy Frances Goff Papers, Center for American History, University of Texas at Austin.*

ranch at Telegraph on the Llano River outside of Junction. Conditions were spartan. Sometimes they would have to cut brush before the hunt could begin. Stevenson rose early, sometimes at four in the morning in his cold stone house. He brewed the coffee in a granite pot, pouring the water in from the pimento cheese glass that he used as a measuring cup. The governor was partial to "Ten High" Bourbon, and on those chilly mornings he would say to Goff and McDuffie: "Drink some of this; it will really warm you up." Frances Goff regarded Coke Stevenson as "a dear, dear person" whose political views agreed with hers. She called him "the most constitutional of all the governors I knew in those days."

Frances Goff's close friendships with men such as Stevenson and others rested on a mutual respect rather than any kind of physical intimacy. She knew that if she embarked on a romantic relationship with any of the politicians in the state capitol that it would rapidly become common knowledge. In an era when the double standard of sexual conduct still operated, a woman who crossed the invisible barriers of female virtue would have been labeled in a way that would have ended her effectiveness in state government. As the pictures in her scrapbook attest, Frances Goff joined and enjoyed parties that went out to the Highland Lakes and rollicked in the Austin countryside. Nonetheless, she made sure that no questions could be raised about her integrity and honor in the close-knit world of state politics.

While Frances Goff enjoyed the work of the House appropriations committee, she stayed in that post only a short time. Another turn in her life occurred when the Texas Railroad Commission came before the committee early in 1941 to get its appropriation for the next two years. Because Jerry Sadler was a Railroad Commissioner, Goff faced the prospect of the hearing with some trepidation. She went to Chairman Reed to ask to be excused from attending.

"I kind of ran Jerry Sadler out of the Capitol," Goff explained.

Reed assured her that nothing would happen. "You're going to sit right here where you always sit, and I am going to be right next to you."

The hearing went smoothly until Reed asked the three commissioners, Sadler, Olin D. Culberson, and Ernest O. Thompson, if they had any other requests. When Frances Goff heard Sadler say: "Mr. Chairman," she assumed that her time had come. To her surprise, Sadler remarked: "There is one thing that we need that we do not have at the Railroad Commission. That's a personnel director. I want a position in the budget for personnel director that will pay $2100 a year. If you give us that, *that woman sitting right down there is going to have the job!*" To Frances Goff's amazement, Sadler pointed at her.

The new position represented a significant raise over the five dollars a day that Goff received while the legislature was in session. As soon as the legislative session ended, she went to the commission to start work in July 1941. Within twelve months, Frances Goff had worked for one governor, gotten to know a second, and seen the legislature operate from the inside. In her papers, she saved one of the indications of her favored status with the lawmakers. It was the "report" of a mock committee to make annual awards about members including such prizes as the "most modest member" (D. B. Hardeman) and the "meanest member" (Fred Red Harris, chosen unanimously).

Goff's expertise in Texas politics was growing. As she approached her twenty-fifth birthday, she had become an Austin insider, one of the people who mattered in the close-knit world of state government. The phrase "Ask Frances" when a legislator wanted something done was becoming as common around the Texas legislature in the early 1940s as it would be at M. D. Anderson Hospital and the Bluebonnet Girls State program in the decades ahead.

Chapter 3

Sergeant Goff

Frances Goff began work at the Texas Railroad Commission during the summer of 1941. One of the most powerful agencies of state government, the commission had been founded in 1891 to oversee the state's rail lines. Its mandate had expanded to include the oil industry by 1919. Since Texas was a major source of American oil production during the 1940s, the policies of the Railroad Commission had a significant impact on the price of energy in the United States and around the world.

Of the three commissioners, Ernest O. Thompson was the best known. He had run for governor and had an international reputation for his role with the commission. "Colonel" Thompson struck Frances Goff as being egotistical. His secretary resented Goff and made life as unpleasant for her as possible. Olin Culberson was another matter. Behind his grumpy and rough facade, Goff found him basically a gentle person.

Jerry Sadler was the character of the commission. He instructed Goff and the other employees that they could not date anyone who worked at the commission. He told the staff that they were to work each day, go home at night, and forget about their co-workers in a social sense. Goff found it ironic that Sadler had then installed a woman whom he was dating in a job at the commission. Sadler and his friend were not married until September 1942.

Frances Goff's duties at the commission did not involve policy issues. Her task was to resolve personnel issues, which she deemed confused and chaotic. Each commissioner had so many positions within the agency. In the process of parceling out the openings, it often became unclear where particular individuals stood within the commission's structure. Goff attempted to introduce some order into the hiring practices, and she often discharged the duties of the secretary of the commission when he was away. She performed her responsibilities with her usual efficiency, but the work at the commission did not challenge her executive abilities.

America's entry into World War II in December 1941 brought another abrupt change in Frances Goff's career. After the Japanese attack on Pearl Harbor, Jerry Sadler told President Franklin D. Roosevelt that he planned to resign from the commission to join the armed forces in six months. Sadler was in his mid-thirties, had a weight problem, and moved on a plastic hip, but he was determined to serve his country. In May 1942, Sadler informed the press of his resignation plans. With a vacancy impending, Governor Stevenson decided not to appoint an interim commissioner. Instead, an election to replace Sadler became part of the Democratic primary in June 1942.

The winner of the primary was Beauford H. Jester. A native of Corsicana, Jester attended the University of Texas where he was active in the Kappa Sigma fraternity and sang in the glee club. He made a fortune practicing law in the oil industry representing such prominent and controversial firms as Magnolia Oil. Jester also acquired a well-deserved reputation as a "playboy." His taste for beautiful female companions became a byword in Texas politics.

When Jester knew that the election had been won, he spoke with Coke Stevenson about the commission employees and their future. The governor anticipated that Jester would take his patronage views into account since Stevenson's decision about the 1942 elections had made Jester's election to the commission possible. As Coke Stevenson later related the conversation to Frances Goff, he said to Jester: "I have one person in whom I am interested over there, Frances Goff."

Jester assured Stevenson: "I'll take care of it."

And so he did, but in a manner that became characteristic of Jester's political style. Frances Goff soon found that she had been fired. Jester had a mistress and searched for a space for her on the commission staff. He eyed the post of personnel director, which was as a well-paying slot. So out went Frances Goff on November 1, 1942, and in came Jester's favorite. The episode affected Goff's future relations with Jester when he became governor in 1947. For the moment, however, she was once again out of a job.

When Frances informed Coke Stevenson of what had happened to her, the governor telephoned Weaver Baker at the State Board of Control. Weaver Baker had been the governor's law partner in Junction before becoming head of the powerful state agency. Baker asked Goff to go to work for him right away. Her official title was Chief Claims Auditor for State Hospitals and Special Schools. The change from the Railroad Commission to the Board of

Control introduced her to the work on state budgets that she would be doing for most of the ensuing decade.

The Texas Board of Control no longer exists; the General Services Commission has replaced it. In the 1940s, however, its role was to prepare the governor's budget, to do the purchasing, and to oversee the state's eleemosynary institutions. These included the various state schools, such as the School for the Blind (now the School for the Blind and Visually Impaired), the School for the Deaf, and the Confederate Home, all of which are in Austin. In fact, Goff's job at the Board of Control was to visit each of the state institutions and measure their buildings to see how much available space they contained.

The work of the board suited Frances Goff's abilities, and she rapidly displayed an impressive aptitude for budget issues. She mastered the inner workings of "the big book," the volume-sized state budget and the array of numbers that went into the appropriations process. She also possessed the indispensable gift of not gossiping about her work, and that led the male politicians to trust her with even more inside knowledge.

Frances Goff worked full time with the Board of Control for three months until the 1943 legislative session got underway. She was dining one evening in the Driskill Hotel when Sen. Weaver Moore, the chair of the powerful Senate Finance Committee, saw her. He told Goff that he did not have anyone to work for him during the session, and he needed to find available office space as well. "Can you help me any?" he asked her. A tradition of "asking Frances" for help with such logistical matters was already developing within the Texas legislature.

Goff readily agreed to accept the position if Weaver Baker would let her take time from her job at the Board of Control. The arrangement was quickly made, and she was back in the legislature once again. Over the course of the next several months, she handled the routine of Moore's senatorial office. As it happened, one of the senator's close friends was another lawmaker named Allan Shivers. Frances Goff had first met Shivers in 1937. By the mid-1940s, he was one of the rising young politicians in the state. Raised in Port Arthur, he had labored in the oil refineries to earn enough money to attend the University of Texas. He won an election to be president of the student body and used that as a springboard to a political career. During the late 1930s he married the daughter of a wealthy South Texas family.

Shivers had been elected to the Senate in 1934 at the age of twenty-seven and was reelected in 1938 and 1942. With World War II on, he wanted to enter the armed services. He applied for a commission as a military government

41

Gov. Allan Shivers, autographed "With Cordial Regards, Allan Shivers Jan. 11, 1950."
*CN 08961. Courtesy Frances Goff Papers, Center for American History, University of
Texas at Austin.*

officer for captured enemy territory. His orders to report for duty came in
early 1943 while the legislature was in session. After he joined the army and
was stationed in Virginia, Frances Goff received a wire from him asking her to
get him some shoes. Shivers had very big feet, and the army did not have the
right size for him. Frances scoured Austin's hunting supply stores until she
found shoes big enough for Shivers.

With the war raging, Frances Goff wanted to make her personal contribution to her country's cause. She had been involved as a volunteer since 1941
when she joined the American Women's Voluntary Services (AWVS). The
organization was started by Alice Throckmorton McLean in New York City
in January 1940. McLean based her idea on the Women's Voluntary Services
in Great Britain. Her goal was to have a trained group of women who could
drive ambulances and provide emergency assistance when war occurred.
Participants were required to complete fifty hours of training before they
could go to work.

Frances Goff with the American Women's Voluntary Services. Left to right: Martha Lingle, Viola Mason, Lurleen Hubert, Catherine Boles, Ethel Kilgore, Clara Schieffer, Frances Goff, Elsie Crausby, and Lorraine Koch. *CN 08942. Courtesy Frances Goff Papers, Center for American History, University of Texas at Austin.*

Despite criticism from those opposed to American aid for Great Britain that AWVS was not neutral, the idea for women to provide these voluntary duties caught on across the country. By 1942, a quarter of a million women were involved in AWVS programs under the motto "Unite and Serve." Texas women organized branches in Galveston and Austin. To Frances Goff, the AWVS seemed the ideal way to do something to help win the war. She obtained the needed three letters of recommendation, put in the fifty hours, and was admitted as a member.

They trained two nights a week at Camp Mabry, headquarters of the Texas National Guard in Austin. They learned how to drive trucks, how to repair them, and other military needs for drivers. On weekends they went to San Antonio where they took vehicles off the assembly line and drove them to break them in for military use. Their continuing purpose was to do things that freed male soldiers to perform other duties.

Frances Goff's personal papers contain a newspaper clipping from that period about her AWVS activities. She and three Austin colleagues were part of a sixty-four-vehicle convoy of jeeps that drove from San Antonio to Austin and back again one Sunday morning. They finished the trek "practically incognito" because "their faces were caked with dirt beyond recognition." The reporter noted that Frances Goff "nearly took a forced landing when her jeep gave an extra bounce." The verdict was that "Keeping up with Austin lassies in war work gets pretty lively when they take to jeep transport."

The woman who headed the Motor Corps was named Ethel Kilgore. She had Frances Goff and the other women do close order drill and other military training to prepare them for active service if that became possible for women. Frances Goff soon demonstrated her leadership abilities. She rose to the rank of lieutenant and served as financial officer and recording secretary. Goff realized that military life suited her, and she began to consider the option of entering the armed services herself. As early as October 1942, Goff applied for an appointment with the Women's Reserve in the navy. Governor Stevenson wrote to the navy that she was "qualified to render worthwhile service in your organization" and Speaker Homer Leonard said that she was "a young woman of unusual ability and intelligence and of good moral character." Goff saved these testimonials to what she had achieved in state government.

The possibility of joining the navy ended when Frances found that her uncle and his family were having severe personal difficulties. With her relatives to take care of during 1943, she did not pursue the navy option further. Instead, on June 22, 1944, Frances Goff enlisted in the Women's Army Corps (WAC) as a private.

By the time that Goff entered the army, the WAC had come a long way from its pre-war origins. Cong. Edith Nourse Rogers of Massachusetts had introduced a bill for a women's auxiliary service in 1941, before Pearl

Harbor. Once war broke out, Congress and the War Department recognized that women could perform jobs in military service and provide more men for combat service. The legislation was passed in May 1942, and Oveta Culp Hobby became the first director of the Women's Army Auxiliary Corps (WAAC) on May 16, 1942. She told the press: "You have said the Army needs the Corps. That is enough for me."

One of Hobby's aides was a woman named Velma Solé, the wife of Horace Solé whom Frances Goff had known at the Railroad Commission where he served as an examiner. In the early days of the WAAC, one of the issues that the new organization faced was working out a reliable aptitude test to find out which women would be suitable for acceptance. Velma Solé asked Goff if she would take the examination on a trial basis. Her experience demonstrated that the test badly needed refinement. Goff was one of the small number who passed the examination. However, the experience heightened her interest in joining the military. She looked into the possibility of obtaining a commission in the WAAC, but that did not work out. She decided just to enlist and go on from there.

By 1944 Congress had enacted legislation to transform the WAAC into the Women's Army Corps. Instead of being attached to the army as a kind of quasi-volunteer unit, the women were now in the army itself, subject to military rules and eligible for all relevant military benefits. One of the changes that resulted allowed the Army Air Force to promise enlistees that they could have the job assignments they wanted and could serve at bases in their home states. That meant that Goff could perform her duties close to her home and family.

Frances Goff traveled to the recruiting office at Camp Swift in Texas on June 22, 1944, and entered the WAC. After her enlistment, Goff went to see Governor Stevenson to give him her news. His response was: "Well, you're not going to do that." She then told him that "there's not much I can do about it now. I've already raised my hand said I would." When the governor said that he would call the army and have them reconsider, Goff told him: "No, you're not going to do that. I want to do this."

She did her basic training at the WAC installation at Fort Oglethorpe, Georgia. The routine of military indoctrination was rigorous, and Goff later called it "one of the more horrible experiences of my career." The women donned khaki underwear, which few of them had worn. Trainees assigned to KP duty used a seersucker fatigue dress that came complete with bloomers. The soldiers arose at 5:30 A.M. six mornings a week; on Sundays they could sleep until 7:30. Since Frances Goff was "not a morning person," getting up

Frances Goff and Col. William M. Lanagan. *CN 08938. Courtesy Frances Goff Papers, Center for American History, University of Texas at Austin.*

early was the hardest aspect of military service. By the evening, she was exhausted. Describing basic training half a century later, she said: "I'd get up in the morning and put my feelings on the bed and my hat on my head, and get on with it."

In fact, Goff took readily to the military life. Its organization and structure appealed to her, and the clear lines of authority enabled her to work with great efficiency. Her own talents at managing the flow of paperwork soon caught the eye of her superiors. For the patriotic Goff, her years in the Army Air Corps were some of the most rewarding of her life.

By early September 1944, Frances Goff was assigned to the WAC detachment at the Fifth Ferrying Group of the Air Transport Command at Love Field in Dallas. A newspaper report that Frances saved from the Austin *Statesman* during this period described her and a friend, Ruth Raney, as "standing on first one foot and then the other while waiting for overseas assignments for which they are 'up.'" The reporter described Frances Goff as "mildly athletic." The overseas assignment did not come through, but she enjoyed her service in Dallas. Her first job was as a clerk-typist in the Squadron Orderly Room. The office had separate doors for enlisted personnel and officers, and the two ranks never encountered each other in the course of daily business. The commander of the group rated her performance as "excellent" in February 1945 and recommended her for the officer candidate school of the WACs.

On May 8, 1945, the day that the fighting ended in Europe, Frances Goff's life took another unexpected and productive turn. Into the office where the enlisted men and women were working walked Col. William M. Lanagan, who had just arrived to take over command of the Group. He asked to see Private Goff and summoned her into a room occupied by one of the officers. There he told her that he wanted her to be his secretary. Studying her personnel file about her experiences in state government, he concluded that she was an ideal choice. "When I read your experiences and the things you had done, you were the one I wanted," Lanagan said. Frances Goff readily agreed to work for the personable and pleasant Lanagan.

Her duties with Colonel Lanagan transformed Goff's situation on the base. He requisitioned a little white jeep for her which she used to take the colonel and other officers around the base. She had to get up at 4:00 A.M. and pick up the jeep from the motor pool. She then read the communications that came in overnight to be ready to brief the colonel in the morning.

The operation that Lanagan ran was one of the larger bases of the Air Transport Command. Some 500 people worked directly under him directing the movement of aircraft across the southwestern United States. Lanagan often turned to Goff when issues arose, as they regularly did, bearing on Love Field's relations with state government. She used her contacts with Coke Stevenson's office, particularly Margaret McDuffie, to get around problems of red tape. Lanagan said publicly about Goff: "I don't know how my office would function without her."

Goff's new status and the rapid promotions she received from Lanagan produced personal problems for her. The commanding officer of the WAC detachment was Lt. Laura Gwyer. Originally friendly with Frances Goff, Gwyer expressed resentment when the appointment from Lanagan put Goff closer to the colonel than she was. Tension soon mounted as Gwyer subjected Goff to frequent reprimands and public scoldings. The discipline that Goff faced became the talk of the women in the Group. Her friends even gave her a mock list of written petty complaints about alleged misbehavior that conveyed jocular reprimands "just for general principles as we don't like your face."

Colonel Lanagan could not directly interfere in WAC discipline. He told Frances Goff that Gwyer "is going to be affected by what you do, but if she says anything to you just stand there and mentally thumb your nose at her." Goff kept a news clipping of the third anniversary of the formation of the

Col. William M. Lanagan. Photograph signed "To Staff Sgt. Frances Goff: The best secretary I have ever had. W. M. Lanagan Col. A.E." *CN 08936. Courtesy Frances Goff Papers, Center for American History, University of Texas at Austin.*

Goff cuts cake for WAC's third anniversary with Lanagan. Left to right: Lt. Marion E. Swan, squadron Executive Officer; Lt. Laura M. Gwyer, squadron CO; Pvt. Frances Goff; Colonel Lanagan; Pvt. Helen Clouse; S/Sgt. Bill Fedderson, baker; and Lt. Eleanor Borman, AACS. *CN 08939. Courtesy Frances Goff Papers, Center for American History, University of Texas at Austin.*

WACs where Lanagan presented the women soldiers with a large birthday cake. In the accompanying photograph, a smiling Goff and Lanagan are cutting the cake while Gwyer looks on with a sour expression.

The friction between Gwyer and Goff intensified until a WAC captain came down from the Judge Advocate's office in Washington. Frances recalled that her last name was Walker and she stayed at the base for two weeks. The purpose of her visit was unclear until she had a quiet conversation with Goff. Then Frances learned that Gwyer had made a formal complaint about her to the WAC command. Walker told Goff: "I have watched you very carefully and I haven't found any fault with you." Gwyer's effort to discipline Goff through regular channels had failed.

Two days later, Gwyer summoned Goff to her office and began an even more vehement bawling-out. Frances recalled that "I just stood there and took it." When she left the office, she was "just livid with rage." By the time Goff returned to headquarters, word of the episode had preceded her. When

Jane Rishworth between Bea Ann Smith and Virginia Kennedy, 1960. *CN 08996. Courtesy Frances Goff Papers, Center for American History, University of Texas at Austin.*

Colonel Lanagan learned what had happened, he picked up the phone and called the personnel office at the Ferrying Command. His shouted instructions were: "Get this God-damned Gwyer out of my command by five o'clock today." By that afternoon the WAC officer had been transferred. Goff had not done anything herself to produce Gwyer's transfer, but her situation had evoked sympathy in the right quarters to effect a change in her WAC superior.

To replace Gwyer, the WAC command sent Maj. Jane Gould. Described as "a fireball of a major," Gould arrived in Dallas and presented herself at Lanagan's office. After a brief moment of friction over handing her file to the colonel personally rather than going through Frances Goff, the two women became close friends. An imposing woman, Jane Gould was a native of West Virginia. The contact with Frances Goff proved to be a fortuitous one for both women. In March 1945, Gould married Thomas D. Rishworth, a radio producer from New York's Radio City, who became the director of Radio House, the broadcasting service at the University of Texas at Austin, in the autumn of 1946. The new Mrs. Rishworth went to work for the American Legion Auxiliary in Austin and served as its Secretary-Treasurer during the late 1940s. In that capacity she oversaw the Girls State program with which Frances Goff would soon be very much involved.

Under Lanagan's tutelage, Frances Goff rose within the ranks of the enlisted women attached to the Air Transport Command. She became a private first class on June 15, 1945, and received the Good Conduct Medal that same month after one year of active service. A month later, Lanagan advanced her to corporal. Shortly thereafter, Lanagan tried to obtain a promotion to sergeant for her because she had performed her duties "in a superior manner." Higher authorities turned down the recommendation, but two months later her elevation to temporary sergeant came through. By the close of the year, Lanagan had secured her promotion to staff sergeant. Goff told the base newspaper "It was a heck of a long year. Anyway, it was a start."

One episode of her wartime service that she talked about to close friends in later years involved the greatest military secret of World War II. In her recollections, Goff said that Lanagan had been informed that important elements for the atomic bomb would be passing through Love Field during the summer of 1945. The strain of the secret and her fears about the dangers associated with the materials in transit affected Goff's health. She blamed the colitis she contracted at this time on these events. Neither Goff's papers nor the historical sources on the atomic bomb indicate when or how the elements for the device were shipped through Love Field. For her, the experience was one of the shaping events of her military career.

With the end of the war in August 1945, Frances Goff was anxious to return to state government and civilian life. The War Department decided, however, that it needed to keep the WACs in uniform during the period of demobilization. Since she had enlisted in 1944, she had to remain in the service until the middle of 1946. Her duties included a brief stint in Washington, D.C., at the headquarters of the Transport Command in the months before she left the military. Her discharge from the WACs was dated July 2, 1946, and she kept the records of her military service for the rest of her life.

Frances Goff remained active in the military reserve during the postwar period. She held positions in reserve units in Austin from 1949 to 1953. During the spring of 1950, she applied for a reserve commission in the Organized Reserve. Jim Taylor wrote a letter on her behalf asking that the obstacles to Goff's promotion, including her age and enlisted status, be waived in her case. Taylor noted that her close knowledge of the trucking industry would make her particularly valuable to the 910th Transportation

Company of the Organized Reserve Corps, which was affiliated with the Texas Motor Transportation Association.

Unfortunately, Goff was nearly thirty-four years old and beyond the age limit of thirty-two for commissions in the reserves. The army rejected her application at least once and perhaps twice. In 1951 she worked in military intelligence units in Austin, and was then discharged from the reserves in January 1953.

The war had brought many changes in her life. Her grandfather Percy died after a long struggle with cancer in late February 1945. The obituary described him "as a fine old pioneer citizen of Kenedy." He had acted as the father Frances Goff never really had, and his hotel business had played a large role in shaping her view of the world, as well as making friends for her who proved valuable in her later political career.

Meanwhile, Colonel Lanagan had been approached by civic leaders in Dallas and Fort Worth about building an expanded commercial airport that the two cities would need after the war. Had he assumed that task, he would have asked Frances Goff to stay with him to make the project a reality. She recalled that a heart attack made it impossible for him to embark on the airport assignment. Goff kept an October 1950 letter from Lanagan in which he described his retirement and transition to civilian life. He had opened a sporting goods business specializing in golf clubs in Pasadena, California. The colonel told her that "the way you and I ran Love Field and the surrounding territory is one of my happy memories of military life." Of Goff's reserve ambitions, he said: "I have a hunch that you would be wearing eagles had we met a little sooner and had you elected to stay in." A few months later Colonel Lanagan died.

The political situation of Texas had changed dramatically in the two years that Frances Goff had spent in the armed forces. In the summer of 1946, Coke Stevenson was finishing his last term as governor, and he named her as State Budget Director. The position was on an interim basis until a permanent director could be hired, and Goff made it clear that she was not a candidate for that position. Stevenson had not announced any future political plans but the prevailing assumption in Austin was that he planned to run for Pappy O'Daniel's Senate seat in 1948. After seven years in Washington, the erratic O'Daniel had become a political embarrassment even to those who shared his conservative views. He was a pariah in the Senate because of personal scandals and he had proved so ineffective as a legislator that he did little to serve the interests of his state. O'Daniel's poll ratings had fallen so low that any possibility of reelection seemed remote even by 1946. The field of possible contenders for O'Daniel's place included Lyndon Johnson and outgoing governor Coke Stevenson.

For Frances Goff, Coke Stevenson seemed an ideal senatorial candidate. Conservative herself, she shared his view that the role of government at both the state and national level should be limited. She did not, however, display evidence of Stevenson's intolerance toward African Americans. Working on the inside of Texas government, she had accepted the attitudes of the ruling political establishment against labor unions, social welfare legislation, and government regulation of large corporations. In time these ideas would lead her, like many other conservative Democrats in Texas, toward the Republican Party.

In the race for governor in 1946, the battle raged between Frances Goff's old nemesis at the Railroad Commission, Beauford H. Jester, and the former president of the University of Texas, Homer Price Rainey. The conservative Board of Regents had fired Rainey in late 1944 because of their displeasure with his liberal views and defense of the faculty and tenure. Allegations of communists and homosexuals on campus, as well as charges that Rainey favored racial integration, had added to the volatile nature of the controversy. Once he had been sacked, the articulate Rainey announced his candidacy for governor and campaigned for political vindication on a platform he called "The New Texas." The race was bitter and vicious, but Jester's huge campaign war chest and scurrilous attacks on Rainey, combined with the conservative postwar tilt of Texas voters, gained him a decisive victory in the runoff.

The other race in 1946 that interested Goff involved Allan Shivers's candidacy for lieutenant governor. Shivers had been able to serve in the army because he had a four-year term as state senator. He came back from wartime duties in Italy during the 1945 legislative session. In April 1945, his Senate colleagues urged him to run for lieutenant governor, and he agreed. He led after the first primary, and then prevailed in the runoff. When the legislature convened in January 1947, Shivers would preside over the Senate.

Jim Taylor had fought with the 36th Division in Italy and France. In 1944, friends in his district circulated nominating petitions that put his name on the primary ballot. He won the election easily. Since he and Shivers were close friends, the lieutenant governor asked Taylor to chair the Senate Finance Committee. Taylor asked her to be his secretary, taking time off from her duties at the Board of Control.

For the next five years, Frances Goff became more of a behind-the-scenes force in state politics. She enjoyed the trust and confidence of Shivers, Taylor, and other powerful Texas leaders. She played a significant role in preparing the state's budgets and setting legislative priorities. In the aftermath of World War II, she joined the American Legion and began her long association with the Bluebonnet Girls State program. Finally, she found that the new cancer hospital in Houston, now called M. D. Anderson, was becoming a large part of her working life. Goff juggled these varied responsibilities with the same dexterity and skill that would mark her long public career.

Chapter 4

R. Lee Clark and M. D. Anderson Hospital

Frances Goff did not have much time to readjust to civilian life in 1946 before she faced a significant decision about the direction of her professional career. A few weeks after her discharge from the military, the newly appointed director of the University of Texas M. D. Anderson Cancer Hospital in Houston, Dr. Randolph Lee Clark, asked her to join his staff as a key personal aide. Goff declined the invitation on the grounds that she could do more for the hospital in her Austin job. The episode brought Goff closer, however, to the professional commitment that would become the center of her working life. She and Clark had a tacit understanding that she would in the future come to work at M. D. Anderson.

During the years that Frances Goff had served in the military, events at the University of Texas moved in a direction that laid the foundation for her long association with R. Lee Clark and M. D. Anderson Hospital. Since its creation in 1941, the cancer hospital project that the legislature had authorized remained more of a grand conception than a tangible reality. By the end of World War II, the Board of Regents and the university administration had decided that it was time to appoint a director who could make the hospital a functioning institution.

Some important steps had occurred between 1941 and the end of the war. The most significant was the decision by the M. D. Anderson Foundation in 1942 to donate temporary housing for the hospital, to provide land for the permanent hospital, and matching funds of $500,000 for construction. The name of the hospital would be the M. D. Anderson Hospital for Cancer Research. A banker and cotton broker, Anderson had been a founder of Anderson Clayton & Co., and had built it into one of the largest sellers of cotton in the world. Anderson died in 1939 after creating the foundation that bears his name.

To run the hospital during the war, the Regents selected Dr. Ernest William Bertner, a Houston physician. He set up temporary operations at "The Oaks," the former home of Capt. James A. Baker of Houston. In the months that followed, Bertner increased his staff and began research projects. Formal dedication of the hospital took place on February 17, 1944, and patients arrived two months later. For the ensuing eighteen months, initial research activity and patient care proceeded under wartime restrictions. By the time that the fighting ended in September 1945, the acting president of the University of Texas, Dr. T. S. Painter, had concluded that it was imperative to select a director for the Hospital for Cancer Research as soon as feasible. The initial hope was to select a doctor with an outstanding reputation in cancer research.

The search for a director would not be easy. The university was under a cloud nationally because of the ouster of Homer P. Rainey during the autumn of 1944. The American Association of University Professors had censured the University of Texas, and the institution had a tarnished reputation within the academic community. To replace Rainey, the Regents had selected Painter who had previously pledged to his faculty colleagues that he would not accept the post. The effects of the dispute took decades to dissipate, and feelings ran high in 1945. One potential candidate told Painter that candidates from around the country were afraid of Texas because the state had created such a difficult and controversial atmosphere in which academics had to work.

The nationwide search began in late 1945. Several local and national candidates were identified. Yet by January 1946, no clear front-runner had appeared, and President Painter decided that it might be wiser to look for the most talented doctor available rather than an expert on cancer. Meanwhile, a letter dated January 3, 1946, now preserved in the records of the President of the University of Texas at Austin, reached the chairman of the Board of Regents, Dudley K. Woodward. It came from Dr. R. Lee Clark who was then finishing out his service in the army. Clark sought "a civilian connection that would enable me to continue investigative work." While Clark did not specifically ask to be a candidate for the Anderson job, his references from the Mayo Clinic and his Texas background impressed Woodward.

Two weeks later Clark met with President Painter to talk about the position in more detail. The two men hit it off immediately, but Clark still faced strong competition for the Anderson post. During the months that followed,

Clark's candidacy gathered strength, though he was not yet the first choice of the Regents. By late April the board offered the directorship to Dr. Raymond Gregory, a professor of Internal Medicine at the University's Medical Branch in Galveston. Gregory asked for additional time to consider the offer. In the end, he decided not to accept. That made Clark the best available choice, with Woodward and Painter now his staunch advocates. The Regents met in mid-July 1946 and officially offered Lee Clark the post. He accepted and his appointment became effective on August 1, 1946.

R. Lee Clark had just passed his fortieth birthday when he became director at M. D. Anderson Hospital. Born in Hereford in the Texas Panhandle on July 2, 1906, he came from an old Texas family. His grandfather founded the school that became Texas Christian University, and his father, Randolph Lee Clark Sr., was a prominent public school superintendent and junior college president in Gainesville. Lee Clark attended John Tarleton Agricultural College in Stephensville for two years and then graduated from the University of South Carolina with a degree in chemistry and biology in 1927.

He entered the Medical College of Virginia in 1928 and received his M.D. four years later. He interned in Washington, D.C., and at the American Hospital in Paris. Clark then spent four and a half years as a Fellow in Surgery at the Mayo Clinic. He went into private practice in Jackson, Mississippi, in 1939 and entered the Army Medical Corps in July 1942. By the end of the war he had attained the rank of colonel. At the age of forty he had published extensively about cancers of the rectum and the ovary, as well as on a variety of topics relating to his work in the military.

The recommendations that Clark obtained from his colleagues attested to the strong impression he had already made within the medical profession by 1946. The letters on his behalf in the records of the president of the University of Texas are glowing. "He has the personality, character, and other personal qualifications to make him a genuine leader, of which there are far too few," wrote the president of the Medical College of Virginia in February. Dr. O. T. Claggett from the Mayo Clinic called Clark "a fine personality, he gets along well with people, has a research type of mind, and, at the same time, is an outstanding clinical surgeon." For Clark himself, the chance to direct M. D. Anderson represented the opportunity to which his medical career had been directed. It was, he told President Painter on February 11, 1946, an enterprise "that would use all of the interest and activity that a physician could expend. And with its teaching, research, and clinical phases, one could very happily spend a lifetime."

R. Lee Clark at Girls State, early 1950s. *CN 08998. Courtesy Frances Goff Papers, Center for American History, University of Texas at Austin.*

Clark recognized from the outset of his tenure as director that his new position would have a substantial political dimension to it. Since M. D. Anderson was part of the University of Texas system, its fortunes fluctuated with the amount of state appropriations for the university itself. Getting into the good graces of Texas political leaders was imperative. Raising money from private donors would also be facilitated if the hospital had sound political connections. At the same time, the hospital had to prove its value to a skeptical medical community that saw a state cancer hospital as a potential source of competition for patients. Some physicians even believed that M. D. Anderson represented a kind of government sponsored medical care that might properly be called "socialized medicine." Attending to all of these matters while he got the hospital into running order demonstrated to Clark that he needed an aide with political insight and excellent connections in Austin.

Clark approached his sister, Jane Worsham, who had known Frances Goff in Kenedy. Through that avenue, Clark asked Goff if she would come to Houston and join him as his special assistant. She said no because: "You don't know a thing in the world about legislation. You don't know anything about state government. You don't know anything about the Legislature. You need some training." Her memories of what she said to him were still vivid nearly half a century later.

Clark asked her instead "When will you come?" Goff responded that she could not come until "you learn what you need to learn because I am not going to do all that for you." She believed that she could be of more immediate help to him as state budget director than she could from a staff position at the hospital in Houston. Her temporary refusal did not stop Clark from repeatedly asking her over the next five years to move to Anderson, but for the moment Frances Goff stayed put in Austin.

Her life there was pleasant. Her circle of friends grew during the postwar years. She had met Ruth Wilson just after returning home when she needed some surgery; Wilson was working in the doctor's office where Goff sought treatment. They became close associates and shared many political secrets. Jane Rishworth was in Austin with her new husband as he ran Radio House at the University until their marriage broke up. One of Tom Rishworth's aides at Radio House was John Rasco, who married Joyce Cole from the Rio Grande Valley. Two of their four offspring became Frances Goff's god children, including Jeff Rasco whose career and life became intertwined with hers at M. D. Anderson and Girls State. Unfortunately, Tom Rishworth's tenure at the University of Texas ended abruptly. An audit found some personal mismanagement in his accounts and he resigned in disgrace.

Frances Goff's first professional task as budget director was getting the budget ready for the 1947 legislative session. She began work in July 1946 as soon as she was discharged. Her personal goal was to submit the budget on time for the lawmakers to have in January 1947. That feat had not been accomplished previously. In place of the older system where one-year expenditures were not itemized, she insisted that they have precise figures for both

Frances Goff with a copy of the state budget in the late 1940s. *CN 08987. Courtesy Frances Goff Papers, Center for American History, University of Texas at Austin.*

years of the biennial appropriation. She succeeded in having the budget in place and a bill written for the legislature to consider by early 1947.

As a result, Goff soon acquired the name of "Miss Budget." A local newspaper observed, in a clipping that she preserved, that "directing the budget is exacting piece of work." It required that Goff keep "the whole work in her mind and at the tip of her tongue." Recognizing the importance of the duties that Goff was now performing, her superiors raised her salary from $2,640 to $4,500.

She became a familiar presence at meetings of the Senate Finance Committee where she oversaw the progress of appropriations bills for Sen. Jim Taylor. The members sometimes called her "Senator Goff" too. They remarked that she did a better job of running the upper house than did the members themselves. She had lost none of her steel demeanor when crossed. Fred Red Harris, now a senator, tried in vain to get by her to see Taylor one day when the Finance Committee chairman was busy. She stared down the volatile Harris and he went away.

Taylor later recalled another episode when Lieutenant Governor Shivers needed a key vote from the Finance Committee to move important legislation along. The pivotal senator, whose name has been lost to history in Taylor's recounting of the incident, had disappeared and could not be found anywhere in the capitol. According to his oral history interview, Taylor instructed Frances Goff: "You go find him. We've got to have that vote. I'm going to hold the vote until he gets here, because if we don't we lose it."

After checking all the places where the wavering senator might be hiding, Goff concluded that he had taken refuge in the men's room of the Senate. According to Taylor, "she went in there and got him," and brought him back to the Senate to vote. The Shivers forces thus prevailed by that single tally.

The Senate members trusted Goff because she did not gossip about their activities and could be relied on to report accurately what Chairman Taylor said or believed. Her political friendship with Lieutenant Governor Shivers also added to her clout. The two shared an interest in baseball and sometimes attended minor league games together. Goff became a good friend of the influential Sen. A. M. Aikin of Paris, the main champion of public education in the upper house.

Frances Goff also enjoyed close ties to the governor's office where her old friend Bill McGill was Beauford Jester's primary aide. Jester had not lost his taste for good living and feminine companionship, and managing the new state executive tested all of McGill's and Goff's formidable patience. She regarded Jester as pliable and too prone to tell people what they wanted to hear. He was, she said later a "strange" politician who would make appointments of individuals to jobs much higher than the positions the staff had recommended for them. After Coke Stevenson, Jester seemed a letdown to the efficient and purposeful Goff.

During the 1947 legislative session, she proved the wisdom of her comment to Lee Clark that she could do more for Anderson Hospital in Austin than in Houston. Her support was central to Clark's efforts to obtain substantial appropriations during his first year as director. His primary goal was to obtain funds for the construction of a satisfactory permanent building for the hospital. Unfortunately, the legislative delegation from Houston, prodded by local doctors, came out against an appropriation of $2 million for the Dental School and Anderson Hospital. Coached by Frances Goff, Clark suggested to President Painter that when a House-Senate conference committee met to reconcile differences in the higher education appropriation bill that an item be inserted making some appropriation for the two medical institutions. In that way, the hospital could tap into the matching funds from various Houston foundations.

That strategy did not work, but Goff devised another creative approach. She allocated the unexpended balance of Anderson's original appropriation, which had been held back because the hospital had not yet reached full operation. She worked out a budget for Anderson and saw to it that they gained more than had seemed possible during the early spring. By June 1947, a happy Lee Clark reported his pleasure that Anderson had received some extra funds, even though money for the actual construction of the building had yet to be set aside.

The following year, Frances Goff turned her attention to Coke Stevenson's race for the Senate against Lyndon Johnson. Stevenson seemed a certain favorite against Johnson, a Congressman from Austin with less statewide name recognition than the popular governor. Stevenson led in the first primary, and then faced a decisive runoff with Johnson in which the former governor was also the heavy favorite. Overconfidence in the Stevenson camp and the hard campaigning of Congressman Johnson made the race much closer than observers had predicted. In view of her high regard for Stevenson and her dislike of Johnson, she shared the resentment of other Stevenson supporters at the notorious result of that closely contested election in which Johnson won the Democratic primary by only eighty-seven votes. She remembered how she had been going to lunch with Coke Stevenson Jr. when the news came that Johnson had gained crucial votes in South Texas that had put him ahead of candidate Stevenson. Racing to the capitol to get more information, they met another political ally of Stevenson's who bitterly told her: "You know what they did down in the [Rio Grande] Valley? They just shot those people down there and just let them cross off Coke Stevenson when rigor mortis set in." For Goff and her friends, the victorious Johnson had won the Democratic primary by illegal means. Johnson's election as senator in the general election alienated many conservative Democrats such as Goff, and the 1948 episode contributed to her willingness to support Dwight D. Eisenhower and the Republican ticket four years later.

During 1948, while Frances Goff worked to prepare the 1949 state budget, R. Lee Clark sought to obtain money to construct a new building for Anderson Hospital. Congressional passage of the Hill-Burton Act in 1946 made federal funds available for hospital construction. Clark launched an application later that year for a share of the $4.5 million that would come to Texas. By early 1948 he believed, based on reports from the Texas Hospital Survey, that Anderson had a high priority to receive at least $1 million. Adding in matching funds from the Anderson Foundation and the state, a total of more than $2 million seemed possible. Clark also gained permission from Painter and the University of Texas Regents to begin preliminary architectural planning.

Political disputes within the State Board of Health led to a setback for Anderson when the panel met in July 1948. They dropped Anderson from the list of hospitals to get Hill-Burton money. Some on the board opposed federal grants altogether; other wanted to allocate the money to other Texas hospitals. After the money had been apportioned, about $1 million was still available. Once the negative decision came in, Clark mobilized the friends of Anderson to write Governor Jester urging him to endorse a proposal to earmark the remaining funds for the cancer hospital. The lobbying effort produced $500,000 for Anderson when the Board of Health met again in October 1948; the hospital also received its request for $1.5 million in 1949.

These successes pleased Lee Clark, but the issue of state appropriations persisted. In January 1949, the hospital had in hand about $3 million of the $4 million that was needed to construct a building. Anderson's request for an additional $1 million gained the approval of the Board of Control. The Board of Regents voted in early 1949 to allow planning for the building to continue. The prospects for the hospital looked reasonably optimistic when the lawmakers convened in January.

As the session got underway, Frances Goff returned to her post as secretary of the Senate Finance Committee. Letters and memos from lawmakers flowed across her desk asking for attention to provisions of proposed laws. Her careful perusal of bills saved bureaucrats from costly errors. She spotted two mistakes in a bill amending the membership provisions of the State Commission for the Blind, and returned it to the Commission's executive secretary for the necessary changes. When the bill came back to Goff, the cover letter, now in the A. M. Aikin Papers, told her: "Frances, I need this Legislation very badly and I sincerely hope that something can be done about it." She took care of the matter with her usual efficiency. During this period, she worked especially closely with Senator Aikin who handled key appropriations bills in the legislative

Sen. A. M. Aikin with Frances Goff and Allan Shivers at a dedication ceremony at M. D. Anderson in 1976. *CN 08967. Courtesy Frances Goff Papers, Center for American History, University of Texas at Austin.*

session. One of the senior figures in the upper house, Aikin proved to be a staunch friend of Anderson and Frances Goff in the years ahead.

The 1949 session was difficult and controversial. The lawmakers addressed the problem of funding public education through the Gilmer-Aikin law which reshaped the way that schools were financed. The proposals were very costly. Other legislators wanted money for farm-to-market roads. As a result, by late March, demands on available appropriations for the legislative biennium had soared well beyond anticipated revenues. Since little sentiment existed for a tax increase, the Senate Finance Committee began cutting back on spending proposals. The panel knocked out of the eleemosynary bill the provisions allocating $1,350,000 for Anderson Hospital and another $2,397,000 for the University of Texas Dental School.

A storm of protest followed these actions. Clark again appealed to the Houston community to pressure lawmakers; editorials and letters poured into Austin. Still, by mid-April a $70 million gap remained between revenue and appropriations. Frances Goff met with President Painter on April 12 to brief him on the gloomy prospects. After hearing her assessment, Painter wrote to a former regent: "In view of the present situation, the outlook for additional funds is not very bright but we will keep working and do the best we can." On May 4, 1949, the Finance Committee put the M. D. Anderson appropriation back into the proposed spending bill. The committee did not, however, find the money to pay for that project or the other spending goals.

Then Frances Goff devised an ingenious legislative solution to the political problem. As she surveyed the situation in Jim Taylor's office, it became apparent that there was not enough revenue available to pay for all the pending appropriations that the lawmakers had authorized. She realized that the bill to make appropriations for the judiciary could not receive the necessary certification from the State Comptroller because there was not enough money in the Treasury to pay for it. She suggested to Taylor that Governor Jester should be asked to veto the second year of funding for the state's eleemosynary institutions in a bill then awaiting his approval. That would force the legislature to return for a special session in 1950. During that meeting, it would be possible to look for ways, including some modest tax increases, to pay for the rest of the appropriations that the regular session had adopted. Meanwhile, the available funds would take care of the running expenses for the first year of the biennium. Frances Goff's initiative on this budgetary matter illustrated the wisdom of her decision to stay in Austin and help M. D. Anderson at the state capitol. Her proposal proved a key element in the hospital's future success.

Jester agreed with the Goff-Taylor proposal, and thus the stage was prepared to persuade the legislature of the value of funding medical research institutions in 1950. Then fate intervened. On July 11, 1949, on a train ride from Houston to Austin, Beauford Jester died of a heart attack. Frances Goff's close friend Allan Shivers became the new governor of Texas.

Shivers was a more vigorous and forceful executive than Jester had ever been. His aides included Bill McGill, who stayed on from the Jester administration, and Margaret McDuffie, the indispensable secretary. With Jim Taylor's closeness to the governor, Frances Goff had easy access to Shivers. She added her voice to those urging Shivers to spend money on medical and educational facilities in which Texas badly lagged during the postwar years.

Goff's position in state government received recognition from the press during these years. "Frances Goff is Tops in Senate Finance" was the headline in the Austin *American-Statesman* on May 8, 1949. Talking of her position as secretary to the Finance Committee, the story quoted Jim Taylor as saying: "the real job is done here by Frances Goff." The reporter added that Goff had "proved that a woman is the equal if not the superior to the men in this particular job." Part of her success, the story said, was her propensity for "a small friendly game of small stakes stud poker" with her legislative colleagues.

During the transitional period when Shivers was taking over, Frances Goff was carrying on her usual duties at the Board of Control. A report to the Board in her papers of her activities for a single two-month period between July 11 and September 13, 1949, gives a good sense of her hectic schedule. She prepared a report on all the appropriations bills that the legislature had recently passed, compiled a list of all bills enacted that related to the Board, and prepared half a dozen or so other lengthy reports on matters relating to state hospitals, special schools, and economic forecasts. She noted that she had taken "two weeks vacation," but did not add that she had devoted that time not to personal rest but to her first involvement with the American Legion Auxiliary's Bluebonnet Girls State program.

Governor Shivers did not need much convincing to support M. D. Anderson and other funding for medical research. Addressing a dinner in Houston in September, he came out for appropriations for the hospital and the dental school. He then named a special committee, chaired by powerful insurance executive Gus Wortham, to determine the needs of the two hospitals and the newly created Texas State University for Negroes. The latter institution had been set up to forestall racial integration at the University of Texas at Austin and in higher education across the state.

The Wortham Committee rendered a favorable report to Shivers in mid-January 1950. In response, the governor sent in an emergency request to the special session on behalf of the Houston appropriations for Anderson, the dental school, and the black university at the end of February. An even greater lobbying drive commenced on behalf of Anderson in which women's clubs and benevolent organizations played a leading role. They flooded Shivers's office with petitions that stressed the need for the radiological facilities for diagnosing and fighting cancer that the new Anderson building would contain.

Among the groups endorsing the hospital was the American Legion Auxiliary. Unit after unit wrote to Shivers praising the cancer hospital. While the hand of Frances Goff is not directly visible in this campaign, she probably knew of a letter-writing effort that impinged on her legislative duties. It is even probable that the drive stemmed from her own mounting involvement with the Auxiliary and the Bluebonnet Girls State program by 1950. The president of the Auxiliary, Mrs. A. J. Breaux, wrote each post urging them to seek the governor's support for Anderson. This surge of activity from organized women impressed Goff with the power of the technique, and she used the same device two years later when she started raising funds to equip the new hospital in Houston.

With the support of Shivers and public opinion from around the state, the M. D. Anderson appropriation passed the legislature in late February 1950. "You have done a remarkably fine job," Lee Clark wired the governor. "I am sure that the people of Texas will appreciate your efforts."

During the remainder of 1950, the Board of Regents awarded the contract for the construction of the hospital in late October and ground-breaking ceremonies were held on December 20, 1950. Three women did the actual turning of the earth for the project representing the Texas Federation of Women's Clubs, the Business and Professional Women's Club of Texas, and the president of the American Legion Auxiliary.

Frances Goff continued to work with the State Board of Control, now as assistant budget director, through the 1951 legislative session. She had relinquished the title of director in 1948 when a permanent appointment was made. As she said at the time, "I had no aspirations to be the Director." When the work of the legislature concluded in 1951, she came to another moment of decision in her career. This time Dr. Clark delivered an ultimatum. As she remembered his words four decades later, he told her: "I'm going to put it to you real straight. Get on or off the pot by September 1951." With the construction of the hospital forging ahead in earnest, he wanted her to move to Houston and become his special assistant in charge of fund-raising for the hospital and other projects. She would be in effect his administrative right-hand working in close proximity to him in the development of the hospital's structure and operations.

Other opportunities beckoned at this time as well. O. B. Ellis, the director of the Texas prison system, asked her to come to Huntsville and work with him. The job in the prison system was less attractive than the M. D. Anderson position, but Ellis wanted her because, as Jim Taylor put it in a 1993 interview, "most people knew that she could get things done easier than anybody else."

Frances Goff consulted her political mentors about the choice that she confronted. She recalled a meeting that Shivers, Taylor, her old friend from Center, Wardlow Lane, and A. M. Aikin attended in the governor's office. Shivers told her: "Clark wants you to come to Houston."

She replied: "I'm aware of that, Allan."

The governor then said: "We've decided if we're going to get this thing off the ground, you've got to go down there."

Goff protested that "I don't want to leave Austin." Nonetheless, Shivers was adamant. "We need you to do it," he responded. All of those present pleaded with Goff to take the Anderson position. Knowing that she had little real choice in the case, she decided to make sure that they would provide her with the future political support she required for success at the hospital.

She said to the assembled male politicians: "Let me ask you something. If I go there, am I going to have ever to turn around and to see whether you're behind me or not?" Everyone assured her of their full support. In later years, she said that all of the men were indeed true to their word, and she was able to count on their backing for the hospital and for her efforts in other areas such as the Girls State program. Nonetheless, as she later said, it was a wrench to forsake the state capitol for Houston. "Oh, I hated to leave Austin, I really did." In her years in the state capitol, Frances Goff had demonstrated an ability to work effectively within the structure of politics to carve out a unique place in Texas government. Although she often encountered the glass ceiling that limited what women could do, she proved ingenious in finding ways to circumvent the gender barriers of the time. By so doing, she became an important force in state government. Now she would be taking her skills into the equally challenging field of cancer research and the politics of medicine.

At Christmas time in 1951, Goff sent out a card with a picture of her dog Missy announcing that "a change has been made since you last heard from me . . . we now live in Houston . . . Miss Frances is associated with the University of Texas M. D. Anderson Hospital for Cancer Research."

Chapter 5

The Early Years at M. D. Anderson, 1951–1954

Frances Goff began work at M. D. Anderson in September 1951. Her title was special assistant in the Office of the Director at an annual salary of $5,400. The urgency that Clark had expressed to have her on his staff at this time stemmed from the recent experiences he had undergone at the hands of the university and the Texas legislature. In January 1951, he had written confidently to T.S. Painter that "while we are far from having Anderson Hospital completed, at least the program is assured and the permanent building started." The hospital's operating budget for 1949–1950 had been over one million dollars, and Clark projected expenditures for the 1950–1951 to approach a million and a half dollars. Then came a disconcerting episode.

In the 1951 legislative session, the lawmakers trimmed appropriations for the main branch of the University of Texas by half a million dollars. To make up for lost funds, the administration of the university asked the legislature to divert a half million dollars from the appropriations devoted to Anderson. Clark promptly called Sen. A. M. Aikin and had the money restored to the hospital. In his oral history memoirs, Clark did not mention Frances Goff, but it seems probable that she played some role in recapturing the funds for Anderson. The fate of the appropriation, Clark recalled, "went right down to the wire, but I didn't mind." He was not that sanguine in 1951, and the incident underlined for him what Frances Goff could do as a link to the legislature and as a private fund-raiser on her own. Resigning from her job with the Board of Control on September 1, 1951, she began work officially at M. D. Anderson on September 27. Only her death forty-three years later ended her connection with the hospital.

Construction for M. D. Anderson Hospital, May 4, 1951. *CN 08957. Courtesy Frances Goff Papers, Center for American History, University of Texas at Austin.*

Despite her various titles, her real job, she later said, was "planning, developing, doing everything the porters were too proud to do." She and R. Lee Clark quickly formed a close working relationship. They were both perfectionists, concerned about every small detail. They believed in a management style that involved moving around the hospital and showing up at unexpected moments to keep the staff members alert. When something went wrong in the day-to-day operation of the hospital, Clark would call Goff, tell her about the problem, and ask her to fix it immediately. The director rarely lost his temper, but when he did she remembered that it was a "bad" experience for those who had displeased him. Yet when Goff informed him that something was amiss, he would tell her with a gentle trace of skepticism: "Now, honey chile, that can't be right."

To broker her official dealings with Clark, Goff won the support of his efficient and discreet secretary, Marion Wall. Wall had "a great sense of humor," Goff said, and was "so easy to work with." They made an effective team in advising the director smoothly. Goff found in Clark an administrator who liked to clear his desk each day. As she put it, only half joking, "Marion Wall, his secretary, and I, were the ones in command."

Goff's admiration for Clark grew rapidly as she saw his vision of a cancer hospital emerge. He wanted his institution to address all aspects of fighting the disease and caring for those afflicted with it. To that endeavor he devoted his prodigious energies as a fund-raiser, scientific administrator, and political strategist. Goff recognized Clark's emerging skill as a negotiator with the legislature. Under her tutelage, he rapidly learned how to persuade and cajole the lawmakers into ever larger appropriations.

Goff's duties in those early months ranged across the many administrative details that occupied the hospital. She corresponded with the chancellor's office at the University of Texas about the correct form to use in listing members of the Board of Regents on a memorial plaque for the new outpatient clinic. She was also again involved with familiar budgetary issues. In the summer of 1952, she collaborated with the assistant director, Roy Hefleblower, in preparing the Anderson Hospital budget request for the Regents. She won praise from Chancellor James P. Hart for the clarity of her presentation to the regental committee that shaped the budget. She watched the budgetary deliberations carefully, and reacted promptly when the chancellor's office asked her for a defense of the budget request in September 1952.

Goff operated as part of a small staff of twenty-nine employees at the hospital. Her first office in the Baker mansion was a converted bathroom. "I sat on a board placed across the commode, got a typing table and a few other supplies. Those were the days before air conditioning, so you can imagine how hot it was," she told friends in 1976. Then she moved to a small, narrow sewing room with mirrors along the opposite wall so that she looked at herself while she worked. Visitors who came to see her had to pull their chair up to the doorway because there was not enough room to fit a chair beside her desk.

At the outset of her tenure at the hospital, she spoke with R. Lee Clark about her growing commitment to the annual meeting of the Bluebonnet Girls State program each June. She insisted that she fulfill these duties during her two weeks of vacation time rather than on released time from M. D. Anderson. Aware of the political implications of all aspects of state government, she did not want to make the hospital vulnerable to charges that its employees were conducting private business at the expense of the University of Texas and the state. She never wavered in this policy for the next forty-two years. Clark saw that her commitment to the Girls State program could have a positive benefit to the hospital as well. The network of friends that Frances Goff developed brought donations to M. D. Anderson, potential employees, and an expanding number of young women who identified with M. D. Anderson because Goff was associated with it.

As M. D. Anderson constructed its new facility, the contracts for supplies and equipment represented an attractive source of business for many firms and contractors in the Houston area and around the state. Competition for these funds produced infighting among the competing companies and occasional claims of collusion in the allocation of bids. These problems flowed across Goff's desk. In the autumn of 1952, charges of alleged favoritism between the architects for the hospital and firms involved in providing furnishings for Anderson came before the Regents. Clark asked Goff to respond to the specific allegations, which she did in a lengthy memorandum of September 24, 1952. She noted that she had received numerous inquiries about possible bids on the equipment and furnishings for the new building. In every case, Goff responded to these letters with the comment that the bidding procedures would follow those she had earlier used at the State Board of Control. She set up a mailing list file and kept a careful record of all the individual companies that wrote to her. At the time of her memorandum, the hospital had not received any formal specifications for furnishings and no bids had been solicited or selected. She thus refuted all the allegations and Clark told his superiors that the charges had no basis in fact.

Her in-house work for M. D. Anderson was important, but Goff's major task in her first years at the hospital involved an extensive fund-raising campaign. One asset of her work with hospital construction, of course, was that it gave access to potential donors within the Houston and Texas business community. From the outset, however, Goff intended to broaden the base of M. D. Anderson's fund-raising into the women of Texas. Following the legislative appropriations of 1950 and 1951, and a $525,000 grant from the Anderson Foundation, M. D. Anderson remained $750,000 short of its goal for the construction of the new building. Clark and Goff spent a good deal of time during the fall and winter of 1951–1952 considering various strategies to obtain the money from generous Texans.

The issue of fund-raising for Anderson presented sensitive political considerations for Clark. Many in the medical community in Texas had suspicions about the role of the Houston cancer hospital. Doctors saw the new facility as competing with other hospitals in their own communities for cancer patients. Anderson's policy of not charging for indigent patients struck some physicians as the equivalent of "socialized medicine." Resentment also focused on the lavish attention that Anderson received in the Texas press because of Clark's shrewd sense of public relations. He and Goff decided that some

The traveling model of M. D. Anderson Hospital that Frances used on her money raising campaigns. *CN 08989. Courtesy Frances Goff Papers, Center for American History, University of Texas at Austin.*

mechanism had to be developed to allow Anderson to raise private funds without arousing the animosity of Texas doctors. The answer became what the hospital called its "memorialization" program.

This approach involved invitations to private groups to supply funds for the operation of Anderson with gifts earmarked to honor a person or organization by endowing a room, equipment, or medical facility. The American Legion Auxiliary, probably with some prodding from Goff, had already launched a campaign to raise $50,000 in 1951. Other organizations taking part included the Business and Professional Women's Clubs, known as the B&PW, and the Texas Federation of Women's Clubs. The Board of Regents endorsed the proposal for a memorialization drive, and the campaign got underway in November 1952.

Frances Goff spearheaded the campaign for Anderson. By this time, her years in politics and her growing participation in the Bluebonnet Girls State program had given her a network of women across the state who would respond to her personal appeal. She was also resourceful in stimulating interest at the grassroots level. Her friends saw to it that she received invitations to come to city after city to outline the needs of Anderson and describe what women's groups might supply to assist in the struggle against cancer.

The primary focus of Goff's fund-raising became the American Legion Auxiliary. In later years, she described the Federation of Women's Clubs as tight-fisted, while the B&PW performed effectively. She knew the Auxiliary best and used her contacts to secure the money that she sought. Her major ally in this campaign was Virginia Bailey of the West Texas town of Alpine. Long active in the affairs of her local post, Bailey was the same age as Goff, and the two women shared a conservative political philosophy as well. Bailey would later act as campaign manager for such conservative state politicians as Allan Shivers, Price Daniel, and Jack Cox during the 1950s and 1960s. She became one of Goff's first important allies within the structure of the Auxiliary as chair of the fund-raising campaign for Anderson from 1952 to 1954.

Frances Goff raised money by an extensive round of automobile tours across the state from women's clubs to Auxiliary meetings in towns large and small. She and Bailey traveled in Goff's Buick Riviera. "We might be in El Paso one day and Beaumont the next," she recalled in 1994. In 1981, she reminisced about the experience and the Beeville *Bee-Picayune* of January 19 recorded her remarks. It was "seven days on the road raising money, then another seven days spending it." She became adept at outlining the needs of the hospital. "We had models of patient rooms and a lucite model of the hospital," she said in her retirement announcement in 1982, "and a special case that just fit into the trunk of my car. I think I traveled over every inch of the state with those models."

The hard work paid off. By September 1953, a smiling Lee Clark received $30,000 from the Auxiliary's president and the remainder of the $50,000 pledge came in before the hospital's new building was dedicated a year later.

Throughout the fund-raising drive, Goff used her political contacts to insure its success. When a dozen citizens in Abilene donated $1,000 for the "City of Abilene Room," Goff asked the office of Governor Shivers to prepare a letter to the mayor of Abilene thanking him for the gift "and mentioning the fact that it is the first city to make such a contribution." Goff drafted the letter herself, Shivers made a few editorial changes, and the letter went on

R. Lee Clark and American Legion Auxiliary president Marian Blieden, Aug. 2, 1953, with the results of a fundraising drive for the hospital. *CN 08988. Courtesy Frances Goff Papers, Center for American History, University of Texas at Austin.*

its way. She also asked that the governor allow the hospital to use the occasion for some publicity that would "encourage other cities to make similar contributions." These documents in Governor Shivers's papers show how adroitly Goff relied on the strong links that she had established within the state government.

She also capitalized on her skills at the legislative process to assist the hospital with its urgent funding needs. She helped arrange a visit from a delegation of lawmakers in February 1953 that included her old friends A. M. Aikin and Wardlow Lane. As Goff put it years later, "I had worked with all of those people for so many years before I came here that we had an open door to the members of the House and Senate."

The Senate Finance Subcommittee was enthralled as Lee Clark explained the hospital's mission. Lane's reaction was quoted in the Houston *Chronicle* of February 26, 1953: "Keep on talking doctor. I'll stay here all evening, the wonderful work you people are doing in the M. D. Anderson Hospital charms me." As Goff said in a 1989 interview, Lee Clark, under her tutelage, had "developed into a man who could sit down at the appropriation table with the Finance Committee of the Senate and just talk to 'em and charm them out of the tree."

Building a political consensus was only a small part of her contribution to the hospital during that year. As the 1953 legislative session drew to a close, she saw that the lawmakers had left an unexpended balance of money appropriated during the 1951 session. Dr. Clark was away from Houston at the time, but she discussed her idea with him over the telephone. Gaining his approval, she drafted what became Senate Bill 265. That measure authorized the expenditure of up to $400,000 from these funds to complete building construction and improve sites, as well as to equip and furnish these structures. Dr. Clark told her to discuss the idea with the chancellor of the university, James P. Hart. She was to obtain his permission for the university to ask the legislature that the bill be introduced in the waning days of the legislative session. As Goff told the story in a 1989 memorandum in her papers, Hart listened to her and said: "I don't really know what you are doing but you seem to so go ahead and do whatever needs to be done."

With the permission of her superiors in hand, Goff called her friends at the capitol and had the bill introduced in the Senate on May 19, 1953, and passed the same day by a vote of 28–0. The House acted on the measure a day later and she was again successful, this time by a vote of 134–2. Shivers signed the bill on June 4, 1953. Frances Goff took special pride in this accomplishment. The appropriation bill that she had arranged in 1950 and the law that she had enacted three years later were the only occasions when M. D. Anderson received funds from general revenues for construction of the hospital. Shortly thereafter, the legislature placed the hospital within the framework of constitutional language that made it an institution within the University of Texas system. That meant that building funds in the future had to be derived from the Permanent University Fund, gifts, or some area other than general revenue. Through her skill as a legislative manager, Frances Goff in 1950 and 1953 had channeled $1,750,000 to M. D. Anderson Hospital.

Amid the professional rewards and pressures of the move to Houston and the new position at M. D. Anderson, Frances Goff also continued her active involvement in Texas politics and her relations with her large extended family. Her father, Alfred T. Goff, had become an executive for Mobil Oil in charge of land development for service stations across Texas. By the early 1950s, his second marriage had ended in divorce and he was married a third time to another friend of Frances's mother in Kenedy. Alfred and his daughter were still somewhat estranged and had only minimal contact during her adult life. During Alfred's second marriage, the infamous Elizabeth had written some harsh words about the Goff family, and Alfred's relatives had largely ostracized him.

Frances's grandmother, Ida Mary Goff, died of a heart attack in 1952. Hesitant about attending the funeral against her father's wishes, she was pleased when one of her aunts called her and said: "He wants you to come." She asked whether in fact her father had made such a comment, and her aunt responded: "Yes, he does, that's the first thing he asked me, would I call you and ask you to come."

Her willingness to meet her father and her energy during the family sadness drew the Goffs back together. She and her father reconciled, and he began visiting her regularly in Houston. Frances took care of her father's personal affairs in the decade and a half before his death in 1971.

Work at M. D. Anderson did not diminish Frances Goff's zest to take part in state politics in the 1950s, and she was present at the events that split the Democratic Party in the state into warring factions for years. In her case, the 1952 election led her away from her previous allegiance to the Democrats and into the ranks of the Shivercrats who supported the presidential candidacy of Dwight D. Eisenhower.

The specific issue that divided Governor Shivers and his wing of the Democratic Party from the Truman administration and the national Democrats had to do with the ownership of the coastal areas known as the tidelands under which were large oil reserves. President Harry S. Truman and his administration argued that these lands belonged to the federal government; Shivers contended that they were the state's property. The president vetoed a bill during the spring of 1952 that would have given Texas control of the tidelands ten and a half miles off shore. That move added to the political leverage that Shivers possessed with conservative Texas voters who saw the tidelands as part of their state sovereignty and the key to their state funding for public education.

For Shivers the answer to the tidelands problem now became the election of a Republican president in 1952 who would see things the way Texas did. Just how early Shivers decided that he would support Dwight D. Eisenhower's candidacy is in dispute, but it was apparent during the spring of that year that if the Democrats chose a nominee unsympathetic to the Texas case Shivers would bolt the ticket and back Eisenhower. The general and his campaign had made clear their approval of the position of Shivers and Texas toward the tidelands.

A bitter battle ensued between the Shivers forces and the loyalist Democrats over control of the delegation to the Democratic National Convention in Chicago. The governor and his allies won the contest in the spring of 1952 and sent delegates to the party conclave who were not pledged to support the Democratic nominee for president. As a result, the anti-Shivers forces, led by former Congressman and San Antonio Mayor Maury Maverick, assembled a competing delegation to the convention pledged to be loyal to the national ticket. An acrimonious fight ensued over the credentials of these two rival slates that would resonate in Texas politics for several decades.

Although Shivers intended to bolt the party in the end, he wanted to do so as a Democrat for Eisenhower and not as a Republican. It served his purposes in a gubernatorial reelection race against challenger Ralph Yarborough to remain a nominal Democrat. Thus the issue of seating the Shivers delegation was a crucial priority for the governor at the national convention. The two Texas delegations went to Chicago determined to obtain approval from the Democratic National Committee.

Frances Goff was present as a member of Governor Shivers's entourage. The Shivers delegation was composed of many of her longtime political friends. In addition to Shivers, she was close to former state representative Ottis Lock of Lufkin, Mrs. Lyde DeVall of Kilgore, and her fund-raising ally for the Auxiliary, Virginia Bailey. As it turned out, other friends in the national Democratic Party proved crucial to Goff's ability to be helpful to the Shivers forces at a key moment in the convention deliberations. The vice chairman of the Credentials Committee was William Hillenbrand of Indiana. When he was not in politics, Hillenbrand headed Hil-Rom Industries, a firm that dealt in hospital furniture. Frances Goff described the company as "the Cadillac of hospital furniture." She was having breakfast one morning with Hillenbrand, who wanted her to come see his company's facilities in Batesville, Indiana, after the convention. Suddenly Hillenbrand interrupted

Virginia Bailey, ca. mid-1950s. *CN 08994. Courtesy Frances Goff Papers, Center for American History, University of Texas at Austin.*

M. D. Anderson Hospital, 1954 dedication. *CN 08745. Courtesy Frances Goff Papers, Center for American History, University of Texas at Austin.*

the breakfast, glanced at his watch, and said "I've got to get out to the convention."

Frances Goff asked him how he planned to drive from the hotel to the convention location. When Hillenbrand told her that he would have to take a taxi, she said: "I think I can take care of that." She called the Shivers suite, and asked for the governor's car to be brought around. Goff whisked Hillenbrand out to the convention and, as she later remembered, the Shivers delegation after that "didn't have any problems." The frustrated Maverick delegates could only grimace when they saw these successful tactics from the Shivers camp.

The Shivers contingent made their political feelings clear later that day. Goff, Lyde DeVall, and Virginia Bailey all had brought "Ike" buttons with them to the convention. As the Democratic deliberations went on toward the nomination of Gov. Adlai Stevenson of Illinois, DeVall put one of the Eisenhower buttons on herself, and gave the others to Goff and Bailey. They then walked out of the Democratic convention sporting their Eisenhower buttons. Shivers endorsed Eisenhower over Stevenson, and helped the Republicans carry Texas in 1952. During the rest of the 1950s, Frances Goff was a staunch Shivercrat and close to the Texas Republicans as well. For the next four decades, she became a committed Republican, though her loyalty remained as much to the candidates she supported as to the GOP itself. Her split with the Democrats lasted until she returned to the party in the early 1990s to help the candidacy of Ann Richards, a former Citizen of Bluebonnet

Girls State. Goff's move toward the Republicans was one that many conservative Democrats made during the Shivers era.

Following the 1952 election, Goff turned her attention back to the imminent completion of the new hospital building for M. D. Anderson and its formal dedication. By the spring of 1953 almost 90 percent of the construction had been finished. The cornerstone was officially dedicated on March 19, 1953, and preparations began to move patients into the new facility. Construction finished early in 1954, and the forty-six patients then receiving care were moved from the Baker estate into their new rooms on March 19, 1954. The hospital staff then began work on planning the official dedication ceremonies at which the Regents of the University of Texas, prominent state officials, and dignitaries from the medical community would be present. The organization of the event proceeded sporadically during the first half of 1954 until a date was finally set.

Frances Goff played a central role in the arrangements for the ceremonies. Among her many assignments was the coordination of newspaper publicity about the event. In 1954 she met with representatives of the three daily newspapers in Houston to work out special editions of their papers that would be devoted to the hospital and its future. Later in the year she advised Dr. Clark about the membership of the internal hospital committee to plan the activities surrounding the dedication, and she outlined for him the logistics of getting the Board of Regents and Governor Shivers committed to the projected date of October 23, 1954, the weekend when the University of Texas and Rice University played their Southwest Conference football game in Houston. By the time the committee was established, it was mid-July only three months before the event was to occur.

Goff took over the task of inviting the contractors and subcontractors to attend. She made hotel reservations for the numerous guests, most of whom also wanted football tickets. Accordingly, she reserved thirty box seats for the Rice-Texas game. She wrote state officials about their possible presence at the occasion, and set up a program about the hospital for non-medical guests to attend as well. Her usual attention to detail extended to having a private plane available for Governor Shivers to travel from Houston to Austin and back again with his official party.

All these careful plans for publicity hit an embarrassing snag when the Houston newspapers, against her expressed wishes, quoted high advertising rates to the contractors and others for inclusion of notices in their special sections devoted to Anderson Hospital. Goff received a number of letters explaining that the firms solicited could not take part because of the cost. Her

Price Daniel, R. Lee Clark, and Allan Shivers at the 1954 dedication. *CN 08744. Courtesy Frances Goff Papers, Center for American History, University of Texas at Austin.*

name had been used in a way that suggested she had encouraged and approved such a heavy-handed marketing strategy. She was "extremely embarrassed over this," and told the newspapers that the hospital could not be involved in obtaining specific advertisements from the contractors. She informed Bill Hillenbrand's company on October 12, 1954: "Please be assured that it was not the intention of this organization for this project to be conducted in this manner." Although several of the contractors informed Goff that they did not blame her for the misunderstanding, she told them that "the disturbance over these letters was justified, in that my name was being used without my knowledge."

Eventually all these distractions faded away, and the date for the dedication arrived. Inclement weather sent the dignitaries and 1,000 guests inside to listen to speeches of welcome from Governor Shivers, Lee Clark, and the president of the University of Texas, Logan Wilson. Goff could take special pride in the prominent role assigned to the American Legion Auxiliary for its fundraising success. Virginia Bailey headed a delegation of Auxiliary officers as they toured the rooms that their members had made possible through their gifts. As Goff wrote to the department's president, Doris Anderson, on October 27: "We had a very wonderful day, and were very happy about the representation from the Auxiliary."

Frances Goff had reason to be proud of what she had accomplished during her first three years at M. D. Anderson. Her fund-raising work had been indispensable to the successful dedication. She had justified Clark's faith in her ability to work with the state government and the Texas legislature in obtaining ample funds for the expansion of the hospital and its ongoing work. Within the building itself, she had shown a superb executive ability in handling the furnishings and equipping of the new facility. Any one of these responsibilities had the potential to produce difficulties in the hands of an inexperienced administrator. Goff had identified the personalities and issues involved with the hospital and had built a base of support that went beyond her personal ties to Lee Clark. The next four decades deepened her connections with the hospital and its future as she became one of the behind-the-scenes mainstays of the institution during its emergence as a national research and treatment center for cancer patients and their families.

Chapter 6

"Ask Frances": The M. D. Anderson Experience, 1955–1994

From the time that the permanent building at M. D. Anderson Hospital was dedicated during the autumn of 1954 until the last years of her life when her health failed, Frances Goff devoted her prodigious energies to the betterment of the cancer treatment facility that R. Lee Clark had developed. The full record of her contributions to Anderson must await the history of the hospital as a medical institution that needs to be written and the biography of R. Lee Clark that also should be done in the near future. Nonetheless, it is clear that she played a major part in the institutional life of the hospital, its interaction with the public, and in its approach toward the patients seeking treatment for cancer.

Frances Goff tried to preserve the record of the formative years at Anderson, and she donated a large amount of irreplaceable documentary evidence to the library at the hospital during the 1980s. To her regret and anger, the staff of the library discarded this material as having little tangible significance. Information that could not otherwise be recovered, including early budgets, thus disappeared. Still, from Goff's personal papers, the memories of those who knew her, and her own recollections, a sense of her special place in the evolution of M. D. Anderson emerges.

Her career broke into two well-defined phases. From 1951 to 1982 she served as assistant to the Director/President in charge of planning and development. Her specific duties included acting as a liaison between Lee Clark and the various department heads, architects, and construction companies. She oversaw relations with the firms that provided furnishings and equipment to Anderson. At the same time, she ran the telephone system, the internal communication network, the print shop, and the mailroom. Her responsibilities also embraced administration of the continuing medical conferences and

Charles LeMaistre and Frances Goff. *Courtesy M. D. Anderson Hospital, Houston.*

symposia that the Anderson medical staff staged to exchange ideas and research about cancer and its treatment. Finally, Goff took care of the various social functions that Anderson put on for the community at large, the medical profession, University of Texas officials, and visiting dignitaries. All this occurred for three decades while she watched over Bluebonnet Girls State and the complex internal politics of the American Legion Auxiliary. Somehow, she found time to become involved in a variety of political campaigns as well.

Frances Goff "retired" from full-time work at the hospital in 1982 at the age of sixty-six. R. Lee Clark had stepped down in 1978. His successor as president of the hospital was Dr. Charles LeMaistre, formerly the chancellor of the University of Texas system. Goff's relations with LeMaistre were never as close as they had been with Clark. After 1982, she became a staff assistant to the president working one-third time. Her reduced duties now consisted of assisting with the organization of conferences, overseeing the program for memorial plaques, the handling of "VIP patients," and supplying information about the history of the hospital. Despite her part-time status and diminished responsibilities, Goff's workload at the hospital remained demanding into the early 1990s.

In practice, Goff acted as an overall trouble-shooter for Clark during the years of their collaboration. Her duties touched so many of the medical and non-medical aspects of Anderson's work that she had a good sense of the pulse and rhythms of the institution. She might decide one day what particular furniture would be used in new rooms and spend the next arranging for the visit of a foreign dignitary who wanted to see how the hospital functioned. Decades later she realized that her working style exemplified what would be called "management by walking around." She told an interviewer in 1989: "the boss's footsteps need to be heard. That's been a theory of mine for years and years. I did everything under the sun here and all my people never knew when I was going to be there. They knew that at some time during the day I was going to show up and I always did."

When she talked about why M. D. Anderson had been so successful, Goff was always careful to acknowledge the continuing support and encouragement of the Anderson family, especially the six nephews of Monroe Anderson that carried on his philanthropic tradition. James Anderson, himself a cancer patient at the Mayo Clinic, was instrumental in introducing Lee Clark to the Houston establishment as chair of fund-raising and president of the hospital's first Board of Visitors. In a 1991 interview, Goff also noted wryly that Anderson "helped me hold Clark down when he had a new idea, which happened frequently." She said that James Anderson's death in 1958 represented "one of the hospital's greatest losses."

For Frances Goff, M. D. Anderson existed to serve the needs of its patients. She admired the dedicated doctors and nurses she first knew in the 1950s. The nurses especially ran their clinics with efficiency and empathy for the patient. In the same 1989 interview, she mused about the differences in attitude between that generation and the modern staff. "I've heard old Hilda Ludlow many a time pick up the phone and call some doctor and say: 'Listen (and she'd call him a name) you've got a patient, get down here and see them.'" Goff had correspondingly little patience with a contemporary generation of staff members who, in her opinion, spent time "chewing their gum and discussing about last night and what they are going to do tonight while the patient sits there and pats their foot."

As the hospital grew rapidly during the 1950s and 1960s, Goff dealt with a host of logistical concerns to keep the equipment at Anderson up to date. Letters about contractors and sub-contractors were part of her daily routine. She consulted with George Brown of the politically powerful construction firm of Brown and Root about the hospital's cobalt unit and its effective use. Brown put his private plane at Anderson's disposal to bring the radioactive

Gov. Price Daniel with Ginger Mead, the Girls State governor in 1959. *CN 08992. Courtesy Frances Goff Papers, Center for American History, University of Texas at Austin.*

material to Houston, but the generous action did not prove to be necessary and the cobalt arrived in a less dramatic manner. A decade later in 1966, she was involved in framing information at meetings of the University of Texas Board of Regents about funding for additional construction at the hospital.

Legislative relations remained another area where Goff and Clark worked in tandem. Their joint efforts facilitated the expansion of Anderson's patient care and research capacity. Space was always a problem, no matter how much construction took place. Shortly after the dedication of the new building in 1954, Clark told the president of the University of Texas, Logan Wilson, in February 1955 "that there is an imbalance in our present and proposed staff and the functional building that it occupies." Within four years a seventh floor was added to the hospital wing of the main building, but even that improvement did not forestall the need to seek additional construction funds from the legislature, the federal government, and private donors.

In 1961, Clark and Goff secured a law that funded expansion of the hospital's research areas in the sixth floor of the building. Gov. Price Daniel, another Goff friend from her legislative days, signed the measure in March 1961. Her links with A. M. Aikin also remained strong throughout the 1960s, and she and Clark both recalled how the East Texas lawmaker would always say: "Doctor Clark, be careful what you ask for because I'm going to vote for it." In 1962, the University of Texas Regents authorized the expenditure of $6,500,000 to expand the hospital in a more comprehensive manner. Throughout the early 1960s, as the hospital's place within the University of Texas system evolved, Goff played a key role in smoothing Clark's path in Austin. Her visits to the legislature were more in the nature of triumphal progresses as staff and lawmakers came out to pay their respects to her.

The constant physical growth of the hospital kept Goff busy poring over blueprints and specifications. "Anderson has had continued expansion and remodeling. There has never been a time when I didn't have construction plans on my drawing table from the time I came until I quit handling those details in 1978," she recalled when she "retired" in 1982. The expansion plan that commenced during the early 1960s was not fully in place until 1976. Along the way, the hospital dedicated such additions as the Gimbel Building, the Research Institute, and the Warren S. Bellows Memorial Laboratory for Cardiopulmonary Research.

These ongoing changes meant that Goff was always addressing the seemingly mundane but actually crucial issues of locating efficient telephone services, internal communications and paging systems, as well as the orderly operation of the print shop and the mailroom. She spent hours insuring that the best kinds of furniture were provided. On one occasion later in her career, she had to allocate a large order for hospital chairs. A firm filed a bid lower than what the specifications called for and insisted that they deserved to receive the contract. Goff remembered how the episode concluded in her 1989 interview: "So we had a meeting and I told them that I knew that their chair didn't come up to the specs. But if they wanted to prove it, they had the chair. I said 'Take it and cut it right in half and let me look at the middle of it.' Of course, they wouldn't do it because they knew."

Goff acted as she did with the chair because of her firm belief that any action of hers that involved state of Texas funds had to withstand potential legislative scrutiny. "The Legislature has been very generous with the institution," she said in 1989, and her success with the lawmakers rested on their confidence in her word and her honesty. She reiterated that theme in speech after speech. "Anderson has always been people-oriented," she commented in a 1981 appearance, "and has had the support of the Legislature and the people of Texas. We couldn't have done it without them." She realized that the fastest way to lose the trust of the politicians and the taxpayers was to settle for shoddy products or to pursue the false economy of taking the low bid without checking to see whether the specifications had been fulfilled.

Goff's attention to even the smallest details about rooms and furnishings is evident in the documents she preserved in her papers. In 1975 the M. D. Anderson architects, Mackie and Kamrath, sent her a composite drawing of a "typical patient room." From the letter it is clear that Goff had back in 1971 raised extensive questions about the quality of the shower seat to be used in the bathroom area. The architects took great pains to assure her that the precise specifications had been followed. Four years later, dealing with a design for hospital and clinic rooms, the firm preparing graphics for Anderson praised the quality of the plan on which they had been working since the mid-1970s. The representative of the company told the architect for Anderson: "This is one of the best projects that we've ever been a part of, in terms of accomplishment of original goals on a lasting and continuing basis. This is almost entirely due to the constant and rigorous insistence upon adherence to standards by Frances Goff. Without her interest, maintenance of the graphics system would be like a legislature without a Sergeant-at-Arms."

Goff also kept a close watch on the daily routine of the hospital. She made one of her periodic inspection tours of the facility in April 1978, and soon had a lengthy list of items for the contractor involved to remedy. They included such concerns as "no room number on C4.R006," the lack of a permanent number on Stairwell 1, and the presence of paper signs at key points or evidence that visitors had "picked at" numbers and letters on various signs. Week in and week out, Goff made these tours as part of her commitment to the welfare of the patients and visitors who depended on the accuracy of the signs and notices that they encountered during their time in the hospital.

When the various expansion programs for M. D. Anderson Hospital reached completion, the institution held dedication ceremonies to mark the opening of a new facility and to honor the donors who had made the growth possible. The organization of such ceremonies regularly fell to Goff. They could be as small as dedicating a memorial plaque or as significant as breaking ground for a new building. In the spring of 1972, she coordinated the dedication of the Robertson Memorial Clinical Laboratories. Clark praised her for "having made the arrangements so ably" for the ceremonies and the tour of the hospital that the guests made. Nearly a year later, the M. D. Anderson Hospital broke ground for the Lutheran Hospital Pavilion and dedicated the new Rehabilitation Center. Again, Clark told her that "Everything ran smoothly which was due in large part, I am sure, to your usual attention to the many arrangements necessary."

Goff took particular pride in 1979 when the hospital dedicated a portrait of Allan Shivers that hung in the lobby of the new Clinic Building. The occasion led to newspaper coverage of what Shivers had done to promote the growth of Anderson in the 1940s and 1950s as the former governor reminisced about the days when he, Goff, and R. Lee Clark had found money for the hospital. "Please know that it has been a personal pleasure to work with you over the years," Shivers wrote to Clark in a letter that Frances Goff saved. "I am proud of the job you have accomplished."

A related task that fell to Goff was to supervise the logistics for the conferences that M. D. Anderson held to keep current about worldwide research into the causes and treatment of cancer. The site for the conferences at first was the auditorium within the hospital itself. As the years passed, and the response to the symposia grew, the meetings moved to the auditorium in the Dental Branch of the Texas Medical Center. By the late 1960s, however, even there space was at a premium. Goff recalled in 1982 that one year the "auditorium was overflowing with people trying to get in to hear the symposium speakers. About 10 o'clock that morning Dr. Clark found me and said to move the meeting by noon to some place with more room. At noon we were in the Shamrock Hilton and have been ever since."

From time to time, the issue would arise of relocating the symposia to other Houston hotels. In 1979, for example, the Astro Village Hotel proposed to replace the Shamrock Hilton as the venue for the lucrative symposia patronage. In a lengthy memorandum to her superiors, Goff outlined the drawbacks behind the lower prices that the competing facility offered. She noted that the Hilton was closer to Anderson, a convenience for doctors attending who had patients at the Medical Center. Handling speakers, expenses, and other routine issues would be more difficult at a distance too. All in all, she asserted, the Astro Village proposal "would be a step backwards and not improve our image to re-locate to a motel at this point." The hospital's relationship with the Hilton stayed in place.

For all of their many demands on her time, the recurring symposia present familiar obligations to Frances Goff as she settled into her work at M. D. Anderson. More challenging were the periodic occasions when celebrities from elsewhere in the United States and from abroad came to see the Anderson program and facilities. During the 1970s, as the fame of the hospital spread worldwide, Goff handled the details for accommodating several prestigious visitors. In early October 1976, First Lady Betty Ford and Lady Bird Johnson arrived in Houston for a tour. The events took place amid the swirl of a presidential campaign in which Gerald Ford trailed Jimmy Carter. Mrs. Ford's mastectomy in 1974 had heightened public awareness about breast cancer, and her brief stay brought out a sizable press contingent and intense security arrangements. The visit went off smoothly. The First Lady praised the hospital as "a great leader in compassion through to the indigent" and for its "understanding of the importance of communication with patients." Frances Goff received plaudits from the local Secret Service office for her help that was "of utmost value and made our job so much easier."

In the fall of 1976, Frances Goff's Republican sentiments made her identify strongly with Gerald Ford's comeback race for the White House. When Jimmy Carter eked out a narrow victory in November, the outcome depressed her and she had "a rather touchy political argument about Jimmy Carter" with her old friend Bill Hillenbrand of Indiana. Goff told him of her regret that "a man of Ford's dedication and long service has been rejected" by the voters. By now, Goff's commitment to the Republicans had eclipsed her earlier Democratic allegiance.

Other distinguished visitors came toward the end of the 1970s. Deng Xiaoping visited Anderson and again Goff and her staff made the occasion a striking success. Later in October 1979, Princess Margaret stopped at Anderson for a one-hour visit. The itinerary was a complex one, including briefings on "Neutron Beam Therapy" and "Interferon" that took five minutes each. Despite all of the potential complications, the princess's stay went as scripted. Goff received compliments for "the smooth manner" with which the visit was handled.

In addition to her formal duties in the hospital, Frances Goff continued to act as a fund-raiser for M. D. Anderson throughout her years of service. One campaign that merged the two main interests of her professional life took shape in the mid-1960s. In February 1964, Grover Renfro asked her if he "could memorialize the room where his wife had been a patient." Because the American Legion Auxiliary had already endowed the wing of the hospital, Renfro's idea was not approved. Determined to do something in memory of

Carylon Trahan and Myra Hester. *CN 08974. Courtesy Frances Goff Papers, Center for American History, University of Texas at Austin.*

his wife, he donated $1,800 to the Auxiliary "for any purpose the Auxiliary felt would benefit mankind."

Using the Renfro donation as a start, the leaders of the American Legion Auxiliary, most notably Myra Hester of Houston, established a Memorial Endowment Fund to support cancer research at M. D. Anderson. A goal of $50,000 was set. Six years later, however, Hester looked at the account and found that only $14,000 had been acquired. Hester discussed the problem with Frances Goff, who had an appropriate answer to the Auxiliary's dilemma.

Goff knew that Peggy O'Neill, a former Citizen and longtime staff member at Girls State, was pursuing doctoral studies at the University of Texas Graduate School in Biomedical Sciences. Goff had known O'Neill since the early 1950s, and she saw an opportunity to assist one of her protégés in a manner that would help other aspiring scientists engaged in cancer research. After consulting with Goff, Hester, and O'Neill, the Auxiliary decided to make a grant of $10,000 to O'Neill, and to use future grants of $3,600 each to aid students in the Biomedical Sciences program "who were pursuing their doctorate degree in cancer research at M. D. Anderson." The Texas

Department of the Auxiliary adopted this program at its 1971 convention, and the "Cancer Research Memorial Fund" was created. During the ensuing two decades, contributions totaled more than $300,000 and twenty students received grants. Fourteen of them had completed their doctoral studies by 1988. Once again, Goff had proved the catalyst in raising money, developing a constructive program, and sustaining its growth over more than twenty years. As the dean of the Biomedical Sciences program told her, "You are obviously a very valuable person."

To Goff's delight, Peggy O'Neill went on to become a Professor in Microbiology in the University of Texas Dental School. She remained an active participant in the work of Girls State as well. O'Neill provided sustained care and attention throughout the months leading up to Frances Goff's death in September 1994.

As a result of her work in raising funds through the Auxiliary and other organizations, and because of her interest in the history of M. D. Anderson, Goff devoted much time and attention over the years to the memorial plaques in the hospital that remembered the contributions of individual donors. When a patient died or a staff member succumbed to cancer, Goff became involved in managing the memorial funds and determining on a suitable memorial. In the early 1970s, for example, she worked extensively on an appropriate remembrance for Virginia Kilgo who had been a valuable employee in the personnel office since 1952 and who had died in July 1970. It took more than six years before a plaque was dedicated in November 1977 in Kilgo's memory, a testament to Goff's persistence and tenacity in this sensitive area of her work at Anderson.

As time passed and facilities evolved, there was a tendency for the memorial plaques to disappear and the original purpose of the donation to be forgotten. She watched over the plaques carefully and was vigilant in seeing that the wishes of the donors were respected. In 1979, for example, Goff became concerned about "our lack of maintaining the integrity of donations made for specific areas." She warned her superiors about one sensitive case. A classroom in the hospital had been provided by the Bruce McMillan Jr. Foundation through the good offices of Goff's old friend from the Shivers era, Mrs. Lyde Devall. After discussing what had happened with Devall, Goff reported her terse comment: "If you do this, you will never get another penny from the McMillan Foundation." Goff underlined the potential difficulties when she noted that "donors and/or family members" frequently visited "the institutions to see the areas memorialized, and all are well aware of the type of memorial." The administration of the hospital reacted quickly to insure that "permanent assignment of space will not occur without the permission of the donor." During the early 1980s, she tabulated all the memorial plaques in the hospital, and made recommendations about their relocation as expansion and alterations of the building continued. Clark's successor as president of the hospital, Charles LeMaistre, complimented her on "the excellent staff work" and agreed with her recommendations.

As a kind of historical conscience of the hospital, Goff also became involved in what proved to be an unsuccessful effort to update the published twenty-year history of M. D. Anderson with another volume in 1984. She collected a large amount of source materials for the project during the 1970s and was involved in coordinating the collection of other documents and resources as the 1980s began. For reasons that are not clear in her papers, the decade-long effort to compile another volume devoted to the history of the hospital did not reach fruition, but the information that Goff assembled will help future researchers reconstruct the development of this significant health and medical care facility.

One aspect of Goff's career at Anderson that did not show up on any formal record of the life of the cancer hospital was her personal attention to friends and colleagues who suffered from cancer. Her home at 8406 Lorrie in Houston became more than a residence or a base for the staff and former Citizens of the Bluebonnet Girls State program. When someone she knew had to receive treatment at Anderson or had to be there while a relative was in the hospital, Frances Goff simply opened her home for as long as the person needed to be in the Houston area. With memories of the Goff Hotel in Kenedy ever present, she ran a combination boarding house, hospice, and outpatient clinic on her own and without any thought of payment throughout her years in Houston.

Her personal papers reflect the gratitude that so many people felt for her thoughtfulness and generosity in moments of personal crisis. A former member of the legislature, Grady Hazelwood, told her in December 1976, after reading a newspaper story about her in the Houston *Post* early in the autumn, "Whoever wrote this article darn sure knew you. At the Legislature, I have heard that same expression a thousand times, 'Ask Frances,' and, by golly, that is just what we all still do. I couldn't get through Anderson for a check-up without 'asking Frances.'" When the wife of a Beeville attorney was being treated at Anderson, Goff smoothed the way for a friend she had known since they had both participated in the Coronation Program for the Bee County Fair in 1933. The grateful husband told Goff that "it is wonderful to know there is someone in the vast and complicated world such as the M. D.

Gov. Mark White with Frances at the occasion of her induction into the Texas Women's Hall of Fame in 1986. *CN 08975. Courtesy Frances Goff Papers, Center for American History, University of Texas at Austin.*

Anderson complex who can solve a problem and is willing to do so, at least for those of us who are fortunate enough to have somewhat of a VIP standing." Frances Goff, however, did not limit her kindness to those who possessed a degree of fame or influence. From the wife of a state trooper to others

Jeff Rasco with Ann Richards and Frances. *Courtesy M. D. Anderson Hospital, Houston.*

even less well known, if a friend recommended the person to her she would devote the same energy and thoughtfulness to them that she extended to the great and near-great of Texas. As Dr. Robert D. Moreton of M. D. Anderson said of her, "her uncommon concern for others is a joy to behold and has been a source of much comfort to numerous patients here at M. D. Anderson."

One cancer patient to whom she devoted particular attention was R. Lee Clark. After his retirement in 1978, he remained active until suffering a stroke in 1987. For the next seven years, until Clark's death in May 1994, Goff watched over his condition with the same thoroughness and attention she had devoted to so many others at M. D. Anderson over the years. As one of the aides to Clark noted on the instructions he sent to Goff describing the care that the patient received, "thanks for being there for Lee." Clark's passing ended an era in her life and in the life of the hospital he had built since the end of World War II.

Despite the pressure of her duties at M. D. Anderson, Goff also found the time to work as a consultant on other cancer-related projects or to advise on health issues of concern to Texas state government. In 1977 she provided insights for a proposed cancer hospital in Bolivia. A decade later, she "contributed her expertise to the Governor's Task Force on Indigent Health Care," a panel created by Gov. Mark White to develop "a systematic plan for providing basic health care for our poorest citizens." During the last decade of her life, she was active on the Voluntary Services Advisory Board of the Harris County Psychiatric Center and the Texas Outreach program that M. D. Anderson launched during the early 1990s to provide, in the words of Gov. Ann Richards, "cancer care and prevention services across the state."

The future of M. D. Anderson remained at the front of her mind until her last illness. She helped her godson Jeff Rasco establish a conference facility for the hospital that would perpetuate the work she had done. One reason she proved receptive when friends urged her to participate in an oral history project in 1992–1993 was her sense that what she had done for M. D. Anderson needed to be captured in a more permanent form. Had the second volume of institutional history of Anderson been completed in the 1980s, it would be possible to speak with more certainty about her large place in the evolution of the hospital.

There are, however, some indications in the comments that her superiors made about her in 1985 when her friends had nominated her for an award from the Freedoms Foundation at Valley Forge. Writing on her behalf, Charles LeMaistre said that she had "helped bring the institution from its infancy to its status as one of the world's most respected cancer treatment and research centers." He said that she had "served as the conscience of this great hospital, encouraging all employees by the example of selfless devotion she has set." Robert D. Moreton, who had witnessed her performance as the hospital's vice president under Lee Clark, concluded that "no one worked harder than Frances to ensure that Doctor Clark's early dreams of a world-class cancer center would be realized." He added that probably Frances Goff "will never receive all the credit she so richly deserves for her unique role in making the UT System Cancer Center what it is today." A decade later, Moreton's words seem like an understatement about the part that Frances Goff played in shaping a key element of Texas health care for half a century from the days in the legislature when Faye Stevenson laying dying of cancer to the death of Lee Clark and her own passing in 1994.

Frances Goff's career at M. D. Anderson is all the more impressive in light of her simultaneous management of a major volunteer program for young women in Texas throughout the time she worked at the hospital. Every summer she gave her vacation time for two weeks to instruct high school students in the intricacies of state and national government at the Bluebonnet Girls State program. The development of that commitment and Frances Goff's role as a teacher and mentor for young women in Texas brings an added dimension to her life that stretched from her years with Allan Shivers to the state that elected Ann Richards as its governor in 1990.

Chapter 7

"Youth Leading Youth": The Origins of the Bluebonnet Girls State Program

Frances Goff's postwar career with the Bluebonnet Girls State program of the American Legion Auxiliary took shape even before World War II began. Many leaders within society such as Eleanor Roosevelt worried about the impact of the Great Depression on the generation of young people just coming of age. Aware of the numbers of youth in Europe drawn to fascism, groups such as the American Legion and its female counterpart the American Legion Auxiliary (ALA) planned activities to inculcate America's teenagers in democracy.

Aimed at high school students, the new programs featured instruction in the principles of government and citizenship through participation in a "mythical state." Reflecting the gender divisions of the Legion and the Auxiliary, these youth training programs developed into the Boys State and Girls State organizations. The American Legion sponsored the first Boys State program in Illinois in 1935. Within five years, the concept had spread to thirty-five states. The Americanism Committee of the American Legion Auxiliary called for a Girls State program in 1937. The first such meeting occurred in the District of Columbia during the spring of 1938 when eighteen area girls attended a National Study Group.

That same year, a Girls State program was held in Delaware, with Illinois, Kansas, Nebraska, and Rhode Island following in 1939. By 1941, half of the states conducted citizenship training programs for high school girls. The states adopted distinctive names for their programs such as Sunflower Girls State in Kansas, the Cornhusker Girls State in Nebraska, and Bluebonnet Girls State in Texas.

Billie Murray. *CN 08905. From Lilian Ware Tittle,* American Legion Auxiliary, Department of Texas, A History: 1940–1950 *(Austin: American Legion Auxiliary, Department of Texas, 1955), p. 55. Courtesy Center for American History, University of Texas at Austin.*

The origins of the Texas Girls State program date to 1941. The American Legion Auxiliary realized the opportunities that the Girls State movement presented and planned for its own program. The Auxiliary's Americanism Committee directed the first two Girls State sessions in Texas. Ninety-four girls assembled at Baylor University in Waco from June 8 to 14, 1941, under the direction of the Auxiliary's secretary-treasurer, Billie Murray, an attorney

Flag ceremony at Girls State in 1958. *CN 08909. Courtesy Texas Bluebonnet Girls State, Center for American History, University of Texas at Austin.*

and graduate of Baylor. A year later the second session met at Baylor from June 7 to 12 with 100 girls in attendance.

During World War II, transportation restrictions prevented the holding of any sessions, and Girls State suspended its activities until 1947. In 1946, the National American Legion Auxiliary sought to solidify the program in the postwar era by removing control of the program from the Americanism Committee and placing it under the guidance of the new Girls State Committee in each of the participating states.

Billie Murray had served as a lieutenant colonel in the Women's Army Corps during the war before resuming her duties as director of Girls State in 1947. As Murray prepared to reopen the program, she sought experienced women to help her make the activities of Girls State more meaningful to those who attended. At this time, Frances Goff had been hospitalized for a recurrent medical problem for which she delayed treatment until after she left the military. Murray visited Goff as she convalesced and asked for "my help due to my knowledge of the legislature and state government. I counseled with Billie and made a few suggestions to improve the program."

The 1947 session of Girls State met in Austin at the Texas School for the Blind. There were 135 girls for the seven-day meeting in early June. Soon after the session was over, Murray returned to the armed forces to help transform the Women's Army Corps into a permanent branch of the military. The following year, an Auxiliary member named Mrs. Howard Hudgins acted as director of the program. The number of young women attending the 1948 session doubled to 202. As 1949 approached, Hudgins suffered an illness and the need for a permanent director became acute.

In the postwar years, Frances Goff quickly increased her involvement in American Legion activities. She was among the Austin women who formed their own all-female American Legion post. Frances used her political connections to insure the success of the group. As the post's vice-commander, she helped plan a dance and presented the first ticket for this fundraising endeavor to Beauford Jester.

As the Auxiliary searched for a Girls State director, Frances Goff thought of her comrade-in-arms, Jane Rishworth. With her husband then employed at the University of Texas, Rishworth was a natural for the assignment. Described as "a legendary, apocryphal, larger than life figure," Rishworth had experience and energy. Once appointed, Rishworth asked Goff to come on board and assist in handling the legislative affairs of the program. For the next three years, Rishworth and Goff collaborated on the Girls State program.

The period saw continued growth for the Girls State program. After a brief dip in attendance to 185 girls in 1949, the 1950 session produced a record number of 256 participants and the total soared again a year later to 316 women. By 1950, the sessions had moved across Austin to the Texas School for the Deaf.

The 256 girls who attended the 1949 meeting called themselves Citizens of their mythical state. They were all at least seventeen years old and had achieved at least a B average in their high school studies. The selection process that brought them to Austin included recommendations from school counselors, interviews with the American Legion Auxiliary, and demonstrated interest in further leadership training.

From the outset, Frances Goff wanted Girls State to be more than a sustained effort to inculcate the values of Americanism. She saw the purpose of the program as teaching the young women about how the political system worked. "We stress citizenship and Americanism," she said in the early 1990s, by which she meant instruction in the legislative process and the two-party system. Women trained in the intricacies of politics and government could carry these lessons back to their communities. More important, Frances recognized

Frances Goff presents Gov. Beauford Jester the first ticket for a fund-raising dance in the late 1940s. James C. Jones, the director of the State Veterans' Affairs Commission, looks on and waits for his ticket. *CN 08935. Courtesy Frances Goff Papers, Center for American History, University of Texas at Austin.*

from her own teenage forays into politics the potential for encouraging some of these young women to consider public service. While the results would take time to manifest themselves, Goff knew the strategy of channeling women into political activity would prove beneficial for Texas government.

The 1949 session introduced Frances Goff to a young woman who would become a central part of her life for the next four decades. Ann Willis was sixteen and came to Girls State as "a country girl" who had "moved in to the big city of Waco." The chance to get away from home made the occasion an exciting one for Willis. Frances Goff impressed her as "the dominant person" in Girls State "from my first year on." Willis ran for attorney general, and thought she had been elected until a mix-up in the counting revealed that she had lost narrowly. Amid her disappointment, she learned that Goff and the other counselors had selected her to attend the prestigious Girls Nation program in Washington, D.C., which included two delegates playing the role of Senator from each state. The program gave young women an opportunity to study national government.

Ann Willis (later Richards) with Brownie Moore at Girls State, early 1950s. *CN 08993. Courtesy Frances Goff Papers, Center for American History, University of Texas at Austin.*

Willis also became involved with another innovation that Frances Goff and Jane Rishworth were formulating. Goff believed that the Girls State program would work best if former Citizens did most of the instruction for the yearly participants. Her phrase was that "youth should teach youth." Young women would respond more positively to advice and counsel from their peers than from middle-aged or older women. It was a crucial insight, but it created the first political problem that Goff faced in her Girls State career.

Prior to Goff's initiative, Girls State in Texas and the rest of the nation operated through Senior Counselors, usually female Auxiliary members who looked upon the annual sessions as the opportunity to gain a personal reward for their service to the organization. Within the structure of the Auxiliary, a role at Girls State represented the kind of tangible recognition that set one woman apart from another in the pecking order of the volunteer organization. Goff was in effect asking these women to relinquish one of the main perquisites of their role in the Auxiliary.

In the mid-1990s, Texas Governor Ann Willis Richards recalled in an interview that the original idea for the Junior Counselors may have stemmed from

Ann Willis and Virginia Bailey at Girls State, early 1950s. *CN 08997. Courtesy Frances Goff Papers, Center for American History, University of Texas at Austin.*

the Citizens themselves in 1949 who said "that it would be helpful if we had some young people our own age." It may also have been that Goff, with her shrewd sense of political tactics, suggested the idea in conversations with the Citizens. In any event, Frances Goff sold the idea to the Auxiliary and the rank of Junior Counselor emerged with Citizens from one year returning the next to guide their successors into the riches of the program. The change provided Goff with continuity between current Citizens and their immediate predecessors. Her long-term plans included promotion of experienced and talented Junior Counselors to the Senior Counselor slots.

Initially, Goff invited back former governors and Girls Nation delegates as Junior Counselors. In 1950, Ann Willis returned for the first year of the new approach. Goff realized that the Auxiliary would be monitoring the Junior Counselors and any misstep would imperil her innovation. Ann Richards recalled in a 1994 interview Goff's warning that the "Junior Counselor responsibility would be on a trial basis. We were going to try it out and just see how it worked. I can remember Frances really laying down the law that there would be no boys allowed to come and visit, that kind of stuff. We had to set an example for all these girls." From the outset, the Junior Counselor program succeeded.

Later in life, Frances Goff told the Auxiliary why her introduction of Junior Counselors had been so important. "I encouraged this experiment because it has always been my belief that it takes youth to lead youth. This has proven to be true." As the Junior Counselor program grew and developed, it provided Bluebonnet Girls State with a constant infusion of new and fresh ideas. The young women who served as Junior Counselors and in other Girls State staff roles as the program expanded formed ties with the women who preceded and succeeded them. These links formed the basis for a network of former Citizens that emerges whenever two women find that they have shared the Girls State experience. Social and professional relationships between former Citizens and counselors demonstrate that Frances was not only being patriotic by pushing Girls State; over time she created her own statewide political network of women. This network may not have been a stated goal at the outset of the Junior Counselor program, but its utility as a source of regeneration for Girls State emerged in rapid fashion. Decades after the fact, Goff's ambition on this score appeared breathtaking as former Citizens developed into successful politicians, businesswomen, and educators.

Goff's reliance on youth came from her life experiences in Kenedy and the legislature. Having grown up in a hotel, she developed a taste for fast-paced action that only the younger Citizens could provide. Anne Hodges Morgan,

Frances Goff in the late 1940s or early 1950s. *CN 08962. Courtesy Frances Goff Papers, Center for American History, University of Texas at Austin.*

a former Citizen and Girls Nation delegate from 1957 and an author and educator, remembered: "You give her a chance to choose and she will go with the youngest person in the room, or the person who drives the fastest, stays up the latest, or is into the most mischief. That's what keeps her young, and she's always been that way."

Goff was emerging as a force within the Auxiliary and the Legion at the same time that her role in Girls State expanded. In 1950, her Austin post nominated her for the office of American Legion Department Commander for Texas. The editor of the *Texas Legion News,* Herschel L. Hunt, told the *Austin Gossip Digest* in July 1950 that "so far as we have been able to determine, Frances Goff is the first woman in the history of the United States to have been nominated and placed in the race for Department Commander." Before the state convention took place in Galveston in September 1950, she withdrew as a candidate. The San Antonio *Light* ranked her as one of the "outstanding members" of the ALA in August 1951.

For the next two years, Rishworth and Goff were an effective team in running the Girls State program. Their success attracted attention from the national organization. In 1951, Jane Rishworth became the national secretary of the American Legion Auxiliary. The choice of her replacement was evident. The president of the Auxiliary in Texas, Mrs. H. N. Lyle, and the chair of the Girls State Committee, Mrs. Edward Meier, recommended Frances Goff for the directorship of the Girls State program.

When the Auxiliary was considering Frances Goff for the position, they talked with her boss at M. D. Anderson Hospital, Dr. R. Lee Clark. He endorsed her selection enthusiastically, and in the first year of Goff's tenure he came to Girls State as a featured speaker. The ALA Girls State Chairman reported in the August 1952 issue of the *Lone Star* that "we feel we owe [Clark] a debt of gratitude for making it possible to have Miss Goff with us."

Clark provided more than just moral support. He told Frances Goff that she should not have to use her own vacation time from the hospital to operate the Girls State program. As she recalled in a 1978 memo to Clark's successor, Dr. Charles LeMaistre, "when I first became Director, Dr. Clark felt I should not take vacation because this was a community service we were offering." Goff disagreed and insisted that she not be in a position where Anderson could be criticized for devoting its staff to non-medical purposes. Over the next four decades, however, Goff did use the resources of Anderson and its staff to assist in the smooth running of the Girls State program. The arrangement worked to the mutual benefit of both institutions.

Frances Goff had no interest in a caretaker role for Girls State. She thought that the program Billie Murray and Jane Rishworth had established worked well, but she had ideas to make it even better. Her goal was to create an operation that had an institutional memory stronger than any one person. She wanted to see the length of the program expand, and she achieved an extension from seven to ten days in 1955. *The Bluebonnet,* the newspaper that the Citizens received daily, had begun in 1942 as a simple mimeographed edition. When Frances Goff took over in 1952, two printed editions appeared. Within a year, there were four issues coming out, and soon the *Bluebonnet* reached five editions during the session.

The main goal that Frances Goff had in mind was citizenship education. In her 1993 oral history interview, she indicated what her purpose had been from the outset. "With my knowledge of state government, I was able to transmit it to all the staff, and we had a highly structured educational program in state government, city government, and county government. Then we just gradually improved it. We had some good people, and we had people that were interested in creating a good educational structure."

The key to making this extended civics lesson come alive was for Goff to assemble a program of high-profile speakers. Her connections in state government served her well. When asked in the 1990s about her talent for securing top-name politicians as speakers, Frances explained, "all I had to do was invite them and they'd be there." It was not quite that simple. She worked hard to line up busy state leaders. The papers of Allan Shivers reveal Goff's persistence. She wrote a Shivers aide, Jack Dillard, on June 17, 1955, to thank him "for bearing with me in persisting that Allan [Shivers] speak to the Citizens of Bluebonnet Girls State. I think after you saw what it meant to them, you can appreciate why I was so anxious to have him make an appearance." Frances Goff had fulfilled the pledge that the Girls State program made to potential Citizens when it promised in the May 1955 issue of the *Lone Star* that "an unexcelled opportunity is yours to hear and meet city, county, and state officials, including the Governor of the State of Texas."

Within a few years, the Girls State program had acquired the prestige among young women of Texas that it never lost. Former Citizens from the mid-1950s remember their experiences in Austin with warmth and nostalgia. They came by bus and train from all over the state. Rubyrae Foster Phillips, who attended in 1955, recalled that "passenger trains were very, very important" and they stopped at towns along the rail line from Dallas to Austin for the Citizens. "What was really a lot of fun was we picked up girls along the way. We knew each other very, very well by the time we got to Austin." The dress of the Citizens reflected the standards of an earlier time. "We were all dressed up," Phillips said, "It was like you were going to church Sunday morning, with suits and hats and some with gloves."

With her usual foresight, Frances Goff had anticipated that there might be some pre-session politicking among these travelers, and she had taken steps to avoid it. Once they reached Austin, the girls were assigned to "cities" within the mythical state and each one was aligned with either the "Federal" or "National" party on a random basis. "We were thrown in there with a

Frances with Maurine Martin and Doris Anderson at Girls State in 1963. *CN 08970. Courtesy Frances Goff Papers, Center for American History, University of Texas at Austin.*

bunch of girls we had never known before," was the way Rubyrae Foster Phillips put it.

The young Rubyrae Foster proved to be an important addition to the Goff operation. In addition to the serious study of government and politics, Goff ensured that Girls State offered a balanced program. With her impressive musical talent, Foster was a natural to return as a talent staff member. Goff reveled in the skits and entertainment that Foster prepared. Rubyrae could play any song once she had heard it, and her infectious enthusiasm in organizing skits and parodies never stopped. One of Goff's friends, Alice "Miz T" Talkington, had been grooming Foster for a role at Girls State for some time. As she told her after the 1956 session, "I have watched you for these many years and ever since I went into this work a little dream was always in the background of my thoughts that someday you could join me in the fun and work of Bluebonnet Girls State."

Goff and Talkington realized that they had made a find who would add much to the future success of the program. Talkington said in a letter from that period that "Frances Goff and I have almost worn our right hands off patting each other on the back right after she [Foster] comes thru with something new, she is a surprise to me as well as I know her, she always carries the ball no matter what the play is." Frances Goff was more succinct. She informed Rubyrae in a letter of June 21 that "without a doubt you were the 'find' of the 1956 Girls State Session."

The memories of the women who attended the Girls State program capture the excitement and enthusiasm of those early days. The exposure to elected officials broadened the horizons of these girls at a time when opportunities for women were still limited. "We really knew so little about government," remembers one participant. "We were so unsophisticated." Listening to the state leaders demystified the processes of government for them. On June 19, 1952, John Ben Shepperd, a rising Texas Democrat, told the Citizens that "you young ladies are very lucky to be growing up into a tradition of political equality for women." Complimenting the Auxiliary for its efforts to supply citizenship education, Shepperd stressed that "modern industry . . . and civilized living have liberated American women from many of the former drudgeries of life, and in their place have created new demands on her time and talents—new demands in the direction of public affairs. The training you are getting here in Girls State is just as much a part of your necessary education as great-grandmother's sewing kit was a part of hers."

From the beginning, however, Goff did not limit the speakers to men. At first the women who came to speak mirrored the subordinate position that females occupied in state government. Over the years that situation would change. Goff took every opportunity she could to showcase women in government and public life. The message was not feminist in substance or approach, but the theme of self-reliance and feminine initiative was there. Frances Goff had no illusions about what it took for a woman to succeed. She knew that women had to be better, but she believed, based on her own experience, that women were better and smarter than men anyway.

In her first year as director, Goff brought in female role models for the Citizens. Mrs. J. W. E. H. Beck, a receptionist at the capitol, Margaret Brand, an assistant with the Civil Defense Program, and Lt. Col. Anne Sweeny all addressed the Citizens. The message about female abilities got across in other ways. Ann Richards later recalled from her years on the staff an episode when Frances Goff sought supplies from the city of Austin that had not been delivered. Talking on the telephone with the offending city staffer, Goff threatened to call Emma Long, a member of the City Council, if the materials were not delivered promptly. "I know that it was the first time in my life that I ever heard an authority figure, other than a teacher, called by name, that was female," Richards commented. "It made a profound impression on me that Emma Long had that kind of authority."

The Girls State experience introduced a fortunate few to women on the national scene as well. Barbara Strange, the Girls State governor in 1950, spoke to the Department Convention of the American Legion Auxiliary later that year about the trip to Girls Nation. During her stay in Washington, "I realized that women in politics are gaining prominence. Listening to Margaret Chase Smith, Maine [Republican] Senator, and India Edwards, National Vice-Chairman of the Democratic Party, I was truly aware of the important part that women play in the operation of our government. It was more than I ever dreamed of."

The success of Girls State in the early years of the Goff era attracted extensive media attention from across Texas. Soon young women across the state clamored for admission to the program. In its early years, Bluebonnet Girls State received wide coverage in the Austin newspapers and the state's major dailies. Often the stories were relegated to the women's section. The Auxiliary prepared sample press releases for each Citizen's sponsoring unit to release to the local paper. In 1953, part of the festivities of Girls State were filmed for the television program "Texas in Review" that Humble Oil and Refining Company sponsored.

The catalyst for all these positive developments among the Citizens was Frances Goff. Even at this beginning stage, she had achieved the legendary fame as a leader that would mark the rest of her public career. The Citizens reacted with awe to this person who embodied a life history far different than that of the average American woman of her generation. Ann Richards declared that "I was a little afraid of Frances. She had an authoritarian personality, and she acted as if she were the closest of friends with all of these very important men who came to address us. . . . But while Frances seemed to be their associate, she was also rather reverential about them."

Rubyrae Phillips recalled a similar reaction. "I was impressed with how readily she was welcomed into [the male] world of politics." Her response to her first meeting with Goff echoed the sentiment of former Citizens across four decades. Frances was "the absolute authoritarian figure. If anyone says they have never been in the presence of Frances Goff and says they weren't a little bit frightened, I don't think they are telling the truth."

Words such as "imposing" and "disciplined" recur in these reminiscences, and a portrait of a strong woman with a rigorous and finely tuned program comes through. "Our behavior was tightly monitored, right down to what we

114

Anne Hodges and Rubyrae Foster, 1961. *CN 08963. Courtesy Frances Goff Papers, Center for American History, University of Texas at Austin.*

ate, and how we sang, etc.," recalled one Citizen from the 1950s. "There was no resistance whatsoever to that, mainly because of the enormous enthusiasm about the program and the quality of the program, and the excitement that Frances somehow or another was able to engender through her passionate marketing of the program."

From the first day of Bluebonnet Girls State, Goff made clear what behavior was acceptable and what was not. The rules were strict and explicit. Citizens could not talk, chew gum, wear hair curlers, and cross their legs during an assembly. These procedures evoked little opposition because Frances "had an audience of people who were rule-followers anyway. We wouldn't have been there if we'd been non-conformists."

The moment that Frances Goff strode onto the stage at the first session, she dominated the proceedings. Jane East Malaise, a Citizen from 1963, said "I had heard of Frances and I was expecting to meet God's right hand when I met Frances. And she lived up to the expectation." Anne Hodges did not meet Goff until 1958. "I had heard a lot about her but I was not prepared for what I encountered, which was a person of very military-like bearing. . . . Hotter than Hades, Frances is all turned out in girdle, hose, sensible shoes, and a dress that looked like something that women wore in the service." Goff took the Girls State program seriously, and she expected the Citizens to do so as well. "It is not a game," Anne Hodges stressed, "It is real serious business." The Citizens acted according to the precise rules of the Texas legislature, city governments, and town councils. They passed laws on issues of the day and debated controversial political topics. The elections highlighted the process. Goff divided the Citizens into the Federalist and Nationalist parties and they ran for local, county, and state offices. Election as governor, lieutenant governor, and attorney general attracted newspaper attention for the victorious women, and often turned the winners and losers toward a political interest that they had not realized they possessed.

Through all of the proceedings, Goff exercised a watchful presence. Her Junior and Senior Counselors realized that she missed almost nothing of what took place. She could sit in a crowded assembly hall and pick out the Citizens with potential political talents with an unerring sense of accuracy. Goff also looked for future Junior Counselors from among the Citizens each year. While she exercised a subtle influence on who was chosen to return in that capacity, she encouraged the existing cadre of counselors to spot potential successors as well. After the session was over, the Junior and Senior Counselors would meet and select the Citizens who would be invited back. Goff ordered that the participants speak freely about their choices, and she

Post-election celebration at Girls State in 1968. *CN 08972. Courtesy Frances Goff Papers, Center for American History, University of Texas at Austin.*

did not insist on her own preferences if the consensus of the group went in another direction.

Not all of the counselors relished these informal scrutiny sessions of the Citizens. Ann Richards made clear her dislike for the need to make choices about who should be favored and who should not. Goff noticed this trait in Richards right away and remarked on it decades later. "One of the things I admired about her, she hated to be critical of people. We always had these critique meetings at the end of the session. She always hated to do that. She'd come yelling into the room: 'I hate these meetings, I hate these meetings, I hate these meetings.'" Until family responsibilities took her away from the Girls State program in the mid-1950s, Richards remained a faithful and leading participant in the annual work of Goff's endeavor.

The Citizens at Girls State soon learned that a small minority of their number would be asked to come back a year later. As their fascination with the program grew, they besieged Goff with inquiries about how they might be chosen as Junior Counselors. She discouraged them from mounting lobbying campaigns on their own behalf. "Don't write me and ask how you can return to be a Junior Counselor because you've already done it," she would tell them. "While you've been at Girls State, the counselors and staff have observed you and from these observations if they feel like you'd make a good staff member they will recommend you and we'll go from there. The job has already been done. Writing me, writing to the unit and asking them to request that you return won't do you any good." Nonetheless, many former Citizens lobbied to become counselors, but Goff carefully avoided any political maneuverings on the part of local Auxiliary chapters and parents who sought the prestige of having their choice become a staff member of Bluebonnet Girls State.

By 1956 the essential structure of Bluebonnet Girls State had been developed. Frances Goff had transformed the vague outlines of a yearly exercise in patriotism into a coherent experience of intense training in the basic techniques of American democracy for the Citizens who attended in Austin. A natural teacher, Goff had worked out an intelligent curriculum that fused realistic simulations of the legislative, executive, and judicial processes with the hoopla of elections and a healthy dose of entertainment and fun for high-spirited teenage girls. The various components of the program provide a realistic view of the evolving culture which middle-class high school girls in Texas encountered as they approached adulthood. These formative experiences of the teenage middle-class Texans chosen to participate in Girls State collectively include rituals of membership and belonging as well as patriotic emphasis as part of the female bonding crucial to the development of the informal Girls State political and social network.

The Citizens relished what Frances Goff had created, and the enthusiasm for the program among white Texas women of high school age spread rapidly. Like all such institutions in the postwar South, the Girls State program remained closed to African Americans, though Goff knew that the days of such discrimination were limited after the Supreme Court's decision in *Brown v. Board of Education* in 1954. A more immediate political concern for Frances Goff in the mid-1950s, however, was a sense of frustration within the Auxiliary about the extent to which she had taken over the Girls State program and made it her own domain. Older members of the ALA did not like the use of Junior Counselors or the exclusive stress on Texas and national government as the subject matter of the sessions. By 1956, there were rumblings of opposition to Frances Goff and what she stood for with Girls State. These developments culminated in 1957 with the only session between 1952 and 1994 when Frances Goff was not the director of the Bluebonnet Girls State program.

Chapter 8

The Maturing of Girls State

Between the mid-1950s and the mid-1960s Girls State mirrored the larger discussions within American society over the issues of race and gender. From her first days as director Frances Goff crafted a pro-woman message for the Citizens who attended Girls State with programs like the Junior and Senior Counselors, the reliance on young people to assume voices of responsibility, and the selection of speakers who conveyed a "can-do" message. Yet the American Legion Auxiliary (ALA) preferred a more traditional approach and, after several years of debate with Goff, removed her as director in 1957.

Furthermore, Frances and the Girls State program endured the same growing pains as the rest of the nation over the issue of civil rights. For Frances, an economic conservative and social moderate, the move to integrate Girls State was the right thing to do. However, her actions occurred against the backdrop of a program that offered a fairly traditional and conservative philosophy of government to its participants. From the late 1950s until the early 1980s, Frances Goff's political outlook increasingly reflected the conservative views of her political mentors since politics for her was more about personality than ideology. Thus the combination of these apparently contradictory ideas—a pro-woman message and support for integration juxtaposed against staunchly conservative political actions—presents several challenges to any formulaic interpretation of the Girls State program.

Frances's early years as director of the program built up to a controversy that resulted in her ouster for the 1957 session. Tensions between Frances and the ALA smoldered for several years. While the introduction of Junior Counselors had been problem enough for the ALA, Goff's plan to promote Junior Counselors to the Senior Counselor role after several years of service threatened the Auxiliary. The Auxiliary women resented their loss of control

119

over the Senior Counselor slots, and some feared Frances planned a complete removal of the ALA from Girls State. Several Auxiliary women chafed at the autonomous manner in which Frances ran the program as well as her military service and American Legion membership.

One component of the Girls State controversy resulted from the purchase of a set of Girls State flags. In the 1952 session of Girls State the Citizens endorsed a resolution providing for the purchase of a specially designed Girls State flag. Several Citizens met with the ALA Girls State Committee and discussed possible designs with the hopes of introducing the new flag for the 1953 session. The new flag, though, was not ready until 1954.

The push for the flags continued in 1954 when Mary Mead was elected governor of Girls State. Mead was from a prominent Houston family, and three of her sisters also attended Girls State. She had recently recovered from polio. While she was sick, Mead, a Roman Catholic, had prayed for her health with the nuns. Girls State was the first major event in her life after her illness. Mead credited Goff with her success. Her election, which was an emotional affair, provided the impetus for creating a Frances Goff Benevolent Fund. She and other Citizens donated money to Girls State in honor of Frances Goff.

Mead presented the fund to Goff at the end of the 1954 session. Goff could not offend the Citizens, so she took the money and established a Girls State bank account which totaled around $1,000, a large sum of money in the 1950s. However, the contributions angered the ALA. The Auxiliary women argued the money should not go to Goff and Girls State but should be spread out through the ALA. Goff insisted that the money belonged to the girls. This gift ignited a controversy that had been building for some time between the ALA and Goff over the Girls State funds.

Girls State always paid its own bills, and, as such, was the only ALA program that remained solvent. On the surface, the financial success of Girls State should have pleased the Auxiliary, but many of the women acted with jealousy toward Goff because they feared the program could never have attained a high level of success without her. As Rubyrae Phillips put it: "You probably had some ladies who became a bit jealous with the success. . . . [These young people] are running this program better than it's ever been run before." Furthermore, for some Auxiliary ladies, Girls State prevented other programs from enjoying their moment in the spotlight.

The donations continued in 1955 and the money was eventually used to purchase the flags representing the United States, the Papal States, Protestants, and Israel. The money that Mead and her successor as governor in 1955, Wanda Sumrall, collected for the Benevolent fund eventually went for the purchase of these flags for the 1957 session. Frances maintained this Girls State Benevolent Fund in the Fannin State Bank in Houston as a commercial account. Her personal papers contain some of the canceled checks written on the account for the purchase of the flags. For people who knew her best, the ALA innuendoes that Frances Goff might perhaps have mishandled the funds were ludicrous. Anne Hodges Morgan declared "She's a person of absolute integrity, I mean absolute. There's never been a problem in the Girls State program, never in anything about money. . . . All this work she does for the Girls State program is all volunteer."

Even though she was not director that year, Frances attended the flag-presentation ceremony. Frances and a member of the Girls State Committee brought the flags to Austin during the 1957 session. As she recalled in the 1990s, "a member of the Committee presented the flags to the group one night when we were there. I didn't have anything to do with the presentation. We presented them and they weren't happy about it." This Flag Day celebration further angered the anti-Frances faction in 1957 because Frances loyalists used the ceremonial flags as a way to honor the former director. Some of the Junior Counselors, who knew Frances from previous years at Girls State, presented the flags. Frances demanded that the flags be used since they had been purchased with money the girls had donated. Although she had no official role in the presentation, her presence at Girls State created quite a disturbance. After all, these Auxiliary women opposed to her influence on the program had removed her as director that year.

A Citizen from 1956 who came back as a Junior Counselor in 1957 characterized the leaders' actions that year as "unpleasant" since they resulted in a different standard for Girls State. Indeed the program in 1957 had a much looser flavor from previous sessions. Only one senior counselor from 1956 returned for the "black year," as some Frances supporters have described 1957.

In a definite departure from previous or future years of *The Bluebonnet*, the 1957 offerings contained articles on whether skirts with petticoats, straight skirts, or full skirts sans petticoats were cooler. Another example of the more traditionally feminine approach in 1957 came with the selection of speakers. One evening's program contained a speech about making teaching your career. Pat Mathis, a 1956 Citizen, Girls Nation delegate, and a Washington, D.C.–based political consultant, recalled that there were "fewer glamorous speakers" in 1957. All of this happened in the wake of a 1955 decision that a

Girls going to the inaugural banquet held at The Tower, 1952. *Courtesy American Legion Auxiliary Records, Center for American History, University of Texas at Austin.*

joint inaugural ball with Boys State, although fun, did not fit with the purposes of their program.

Agnes Bethell served as president of the ALA for the 1956–1957 term. Bethell, as Frances remembered "didn't want to appoint me because she didn't agree with my theory of working with the young people. She wanted all of the older people to be the Counselors." In fact, Bethell had served as dean of the counselors in 1952 when the ALA ladies still held most of the Senior Counselor positions. When she gained the ALA leadership, Bethell turned authority for Girls State over to Gladys Strickland, a resident of San Angelo who shared her views about staffing Girls State. For 1957 Strickland served as both chairman of the ALA Girls State Committee and as director of the program in what amounted to a coup against Goff's leadership.

Gladys Strickland was born in Coleman County and had been active in the ALA for a long time. She was a member of the Church of Christ, and had lived in thirty-eight different states as a result of her husband's army career. Strickland told a reporter for *The Bluebonnet* in 1957 that "the most wonderful thing that has ever happened to me was being chosen chairman of the Girls State Committee and director of the 1957 session." However, Citizens who attended that year recalled that Strickland's handling of the program reflected little understanding of the needs of the teenage audience. Anne Morgan remembered Strickland "just decided [she] should run" the Girls State program.

Strickland only used ALA women in the Senior Counselor slots. As a result of the change in authority, in early 1957 Rubyrae Foster received a "very tactfully written" letter from Frances explaining her removal as director and the fact that former staff members may not be invited for the 1957 session. Frances cautioned the program would be different under Strickland's tenure. As Rubyrae explained, "it was pretty clear Frances would just as soon have us stay out so her group just shied away."

According to official ALA histories, the change in leadership in 1957 proved successful. Goldie M. Bewley wrote in the *ALA Department of Texas A History: 1950–1960* (1963) that the 1957 session "was one of our finest" in part because "we tried a new idea this year and used Educational Directors." Nevertheless, the staff in 1957 was unprepared for the arrival of 360 girls and could not get them registered in any organized fashion. Anne Morgan remembered that "I didn't have a bed, I didn't have a place to stay. I had to sleep on the floor. . . . It was just the biggest mess."

Indeed, women who experienced Girls State both with and without Goff found the Frances product superior. After observing that the 1957 session included "a terrific group of people," Morgan argued "the program is the program, no matter what. The program is a hundred times better if Frances is there and her staff is doing it." Morgan explained the reasons for Frances providing a superior product: "It is a full-time responsibility during the year, and it has to be taken care of all the time." Frances, because of the support she received from her employers, had the time and talent to devote to Girls State.

Frances's return to Girls State came about because she proved a consummate politician. Goff worked through her allies in the ALA and regained her old position as director for the 1958 session of Girls State. In the aftermath of Frances's exile from Girls State her good friend Virginia Bailey, the ALA Department president for 1957–1958, helped ensure Goff's return to the helm. In her personal papers, Frances retained a four-page flyer for Bailey's campaign for Department president of the ALA for 1957–1958. Frances relied on several other women who supported her endeavors. Anne Morgan theorized that Maurine Martin or Grace Baldwin, the chair of the Girls State Committee in 1958, aided the resurrection.

Frances told Pat Mathis that Alice Talkington, or "Miz T" as she was affectionately known, fixed her difficulties with the ALA and ensured her return to

Alice "Miz T" Talkington at Girls State, ca. 1950s. *CN 08999. Courtesy Frances Goff Papers, Center for American History, University of Texas at Austin.*

power in 1958. *The Bluebonnet*, on June 11, 1958, described "Miz T" as a "vital part of Girls State for many years." Talkington did not attend Girls State in 1958 because she had suffered several heart attacks. She had been chairman of the Girls State Committee in 1955 and 1956. Her departure from this position of authority in 1957 had been another element in Frances Goff's removal that year. While "Miz T" returned to Girls State in 1958, health problems precluded her active participation in all but the oversight of transportation, leaving Frances, the newly reinstated director, to "[moan] her absence."

In a June 1958 story that symbolized the significance of Frances's return, *The Bluebonnet* reported that "every Indian tribe has a chief and many braves. In this respect, Girls State is a tribe for Miss Frances Goff serves as chief and the staff are her braves." The tumultuous events of 1957 demonstrated the

Grace Baldwin, Frances Goff, Brownie Moore, early 1950s. *CN 08956. Courtesy Frances Goff Papers, Center for American History, University of Texas at Austin.*

importance of preserving a more formal record of each session, and in 1958, the Citizens began the compilation of a scrapbook for each session of the program. Furthermore, the flag ceremony, which generated so much controversy in 1957, became an integral part of Girls State in later years. In 1958 Citizens used the four flags purchased by the Frances Goff Benevolent Fund. The following year a Texas flag was added to the set. Citizens described the flag ceremony as a very patriotic affair. Nancy Pritchard Ohlendorf, a Citizen in 1964 and a former member of the Round Rock, Texas, school board, remembered that "I got an impression of patriotism, and it was during a time when patriotism was not necessarily a cool thing." Jane Malaise noted the "goose bump feeling when they presented the flag and when they raised the flag in the morning and lowered it in the evening."

Two of the speakers for 1958 exemplified the mixture of liberalism and conservatism that marked Girls State into the 1960s. Bertha S. Adkins, Assistant Chair of the Republican National Committee and Dorothy Vredenburg, Chair of the Democratic National Committee, appeared on same program June 13. According to the June 16, 1958 edition of *The Bluebonnet,* Adkins said that women in politics must "look like a girl, act like a lady, think like a man, and work like a dog." Vredenburg argued that "liberty and freedom become useless unless used; all should either work for a political party or run for office."

Yet even after Frances's return, the ALA maintained the Girls State Committee and responsibility for the program's policy decisions. After 1957 Frances pushed for increased power within that body by encouraging former Citizens to become active with their local ALA chapters and within the statewide organization. In 1961, Goff achieved another of her goals for the program. Goff wanted her people on the Girls State Committee to avoid a repeat of the 1957 fiasco. In 1961, Brownie Moore, a Midland resident, became a member of the Girls State Committee, the first time that a former Citizen served in this capacity.

According to the June 15, 1962, edition of *The Bluebonnet*, Brownie Moore declared at a ten-year anniversary party for Frances's tenure at Girls State that "You will never believe all the things that have changed since Frances Goff became director of Girls State in 1952. You've never lived until you've been a junior counselor, party sponsor, speaker of the house, newspaper editor and performed a number of other jobs all at the same time." Moore recalled how Goff professionalized the program with the addition of specialized staff members for the various jobs. Moore and Goff had become close friends during this period. Goff valued her advice, and, as a result, Moore usually played key supporting roles in the annual Girls State sessions.

Her ability to move her protégés into positions of power exemplifies her understanding of the political realities women faced in the 1950s and 1960s. As Rubyrae Phillips remembered, Frances often remarked, "I just don't like that woman. She acts like a woman." For Goff, women who aspired to the male domain of politics would have to perform at a higher standard of professionalism. Yet she did not believe this would be too difficult because she thought women had more talent than men. It was with moves like this that she maneuvered her supporters into power positions within the ALA.

At the same time she was encouraging a younger generation of women to assume influential positions within the ALA, Frances exhibited increasingly conservative political sentiments. Her conservatism resulted much more from personal associations and contacts both from her days in Austin politics and from her direction of Girls State. She admired the efficiency and effectiveness of Coke Stevenson and Allan Shivers, who for many years remained for Goff as models of how best to serve as the state's chief executive. Furthermore, in her recruitment of speakers she developed ties with several noted conservatives including Clarence Manion, Jack Cox, George Bush, and Paul Eggers. Frances's conservative ties should not be confused with a full-fledged endorsement of the burgeoning Texas GOP. Instead of becoming active with the Harris County Republican Party, Goff channeled her support toward those individuals whom she knew and respected. She did not become a political intimate with other GOP leaders such as Jack Porter and Henry Grover. She believed and taught others, including Girls State Citizens, to vote for the individual, not the party. This advice helps explain what otherwise appears as a contradiction—her conservative ties to Cox and others juxtaposed against her support for integration and Barbara Jordan.

One example of Goff's growing conservatism rested on her reliance on Clarence Manion, dean of the Notre Dame Law School and head of President Dwight D. Eisenhower's Commission on Inter-Governmental Relations. He was removed from the latter position in 1954 for his extreme right-wing views. In 1959 Manion helped found the John Birch Society, a right-wing, anticommunist organization. Manion inscribed his 1951 book, *The Key to Peace: A Formula for the Perpetuation of Real Americanism*, to Frances Goff: "For Miss Frances Goff, with every good wish, Clarence Manion." In 1953 the Texas Manufacturers Association distributed copies of Manion's *The Key to Peace* to each of the Citizens. The following year Frances invited Manion as a speaker at Girls State after having heard his address to the second district meeting of the American Legion in 1953. Manion told the assembled crowd in Port Arthur that "concentrated governmental power is the seed of governmental corruption and unless this seed is destroyed, unless this vast army of governmental 'full power' boys that roam the land is removed, [the Eisenhower] administration will be just as corrupt as the one that preceded it." His remarks at Girls State in 1954 followed a similar line of argument.

The Citizens themselves nevertheless constructed a varied approach to government in this period. In the 1950s, Girls State collaborated with the National Civil Defense Program and, as a result, brought the concept into Texas high schools. During her days in the state legislature Goff had maintained close ties with Bill McGill, later the director of the civil defense program in Texas. Citizens introduced mock legislation on issues ranging from provision for civil defense warning systems, open meetings, standardized graduation requirements, a comparative study of democracy and communism, abolishing capital punishment, to barring federal aid to education. Furthermore, party platforms adopted at Girls State in the 1960s reflect the mixed political ideology of the participants since the girls advocated married women's property laws along with adding a requirement for literacy testing to the poll tax requirement for voting.

Frances's conservatism emerged most clearly in her work with Jack Cox, a wealthy Texas businessman who entered state politics in the late 1950s as a

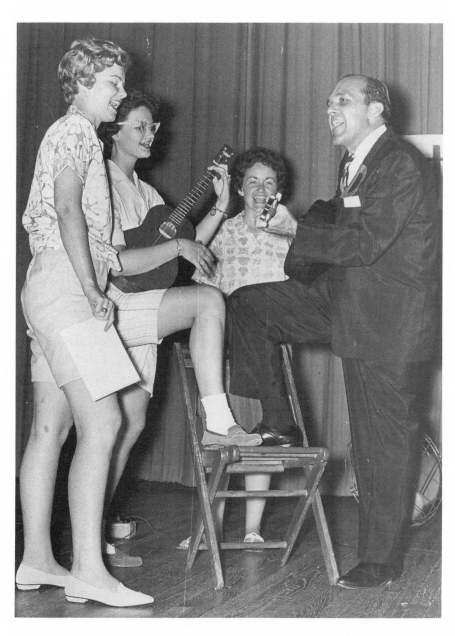

Judy Shields, Rubyrae Foster, Dede Duson, and Jack Cox at Girls State in 1960. *CN 08984. Courtesy Frances Goff Papers, Center for American History, University of Texas at Austin.*

Democrat but changed to the Republican party in the early 1960s. Cox was a featured speaker at Girls State from the mid-1950s through the 1960s. Cox promoted the group Freedom in Action to the Citizens of Girls States and even mailed out promotional literature. He believed the young people of the country provided a great reservoir of strength for political organizing that had previously been ignored. In a form letter to former Citizens dated July 18, 1958, and preserved in his papers, Cox wrote that "for the past three years I have been working on an Americanism program whose aim is to combat creeping socialism in America. This, of course, parallels your objectives in Girls State."

When he made the race for governor in the Democratic primary in 1960, Cox relied on a network of former Girls State Citizens to engage in politicking for him on their college campuses. Frances helped coordinate this effort and supplied him with lists of Citizens. Grace Baldwin congratulated Cox on his candidacy for governor in March 1960. In a letter preserved in the Cox Papers, Baldwin explained that "I am glad we have men like you who are willing to stand up for good government." Baldwin declared that she had no choice but to support Cox since he had done so much for Girls State.

Goff wrote to Cox about his availability for the Girls State session in 1960. In a March 31, 1960, letter found in his papers, she told Cox that it is "needless for me to tell you what an inspiration you have always been to the Citizens of Girls State. I think their reaction has proven this point." On April 2, 1960, Judy Breck, a secretary for Cox, wrote to Frances that "I know he is most grateful to you and to all of the Girls State exes who have been of real concrete assistance to him in this campaign."

Cox coordinated his 1961 speaking dates with former Texas Governor Allan Shivers who, in a May 16, 1961, letter found in the Cox papers, made the wry observation that "a man would think you were running for some sort of office." Conservative themes dominated Cox's rhetoric, and on June 29, 1961, Cox told Goff that "if the nation had 500 women with your talent and ability and dedication, we wouldn't have to worry about communism. I wish it were possible for you to devote full time to the kind of work you do with the girls in Austin." In July 1961, Cox asked Goff for her help with the political situation. He wrote to Citizens from that year who had expressed interest in the sales tax debate and he congratulated those who attained elected office in the mythical state.

During the fall of 1961, Cox made his shift to the Republican Party. In the process he sought the advice and council of James Baker, then a Houston businessman. He also wrote to Virginia and Henry Bailey in Alpine, Texas, on October 5, 1961, and declared that "there is a very strong grass-roots movement building in Texas. Particularly among the young people there is an active effort to straighten out the mess we have been in on both state and national levels." He reveled in the positive response his switch to the Republican party had generated.

In 1962, Cox made another bid for governor on the Republican ticket. Anne Hodges coordinated the push for the youth vote. As she remarked in an oral interview, "we frankly ran it off the Girls State program, that's what we did. Frances was very supportive and very involved in that." Cox received financial backing from young party activist George Bush in his race for governor in 1962. The candidate in a letter dated May 3, 1962 thanked the future president and noted that "the great majority of Texans are conservative and want a change. I know that our present strong position and our hopes for victory in November could not exist without people like you who are willing to give concrete support."

According to the June 20, 1962, issue of *The Bluebonnet*, Jack Cox told the Citizens that "as we sit here, there is a titanic struggle going on between two ideologies. In one there is no God, no Heaven. . . . In the other, the American way of life, man is a creation of God, entitled to be free. One will survive." Cox cautioned that both military and moral strength were needed for the country to prosper. He warned that inflation presented a great danger to economic security. He was not the only gubernatorial candidate to warn the soon to be high school senior about the threat of communism. Democratic gubernatorial candidate John Connally also spoke to Girls State about the threat of Communism that summer. Connally defeated Cox that fall.

The Bluebonnet Girls State program in many ways reflected the struggles that the United States faced as a nation in the late 1950s and the 1960s. Frances also recognized the impact that the civil rights movement would have on Girls State. Appreciating the growing minority voices for civil rights reform in America, Frances determined that Girls State would be a leader not a follower in the organizational desegregation of America. If she did nothing the ALA would eventually force her hand. But Frances also knew that she must carefully plan for the desegregation of the program. She understood that the inclusion of African Americans in Girls State would face much more resistance than the incorporation of Mexican American Citizens ten years earlier. Mexican American integration occurred with little or no debate among Girls State organizers. As early as 1955, Emma Hernandez from Harlingen, Texas, attended Girls State and was selected as a Girls Nation delegate.

The push to integrate Girls State coincided with Legion and ALA conversations over integration of their posts. Separate posts for blacks were numbered in the 800 to 900 range. In the late 1950s Goff told Rubyrae and six or seven other women in the Girls State inner circle that "I want to go ahead of them and start laying the groundwork to integrate Girls State before we are told that we have to do it." She had definite ideas as to how the integration should proceed. Indeed this planning began in the late 1950s and early 1960s. Rubyrae remembered that Frances insisted "above all else it should not be any different." Frances opposed "positive" or "negative" "favoritism" for minority Citizens. She insisted "we are going to have absolute equality. They are going to come in [and] they are going to go through registrations just like all the other girls. We are going to be sure that they are not all in one city. That they are spread out, the blacks are."

Despite Frances Goff's eagerness to move Girls State along the path toward integration, Ann Richards recalled there were some moments of trepidation: "I remember Frances's concerns about how we were going to deal with it. It wasn't that she was going to reject her or anything like that; it was that she knew we were entering a new time now and new problems and she didn't much like it." Richards had encountered an integrated Girls Nation in 1949 when she was selected to represent Texas in Washington. A photograph in her hometown newspaper showed a young Ann Willis seated next to an African American girl. While that episode seemed perfectly normal to Willis, some local Wacoans questioned the incident. Frances realized that the questions some Texans had about race in the late 1940s continued into the early 1960s, so she planned her strategy carefully.

She used former Citizens who supported integration to ensure that the measure passed the more staid ALA, which would have to give the final approval for the change. Bea Ann Smith, a Citizen in 1960 and later a justice on the Third District Court of Appeals in Texas, played a key role in the integration process. During her Citizen year, Smith ran for several offices without success but was selected as a Girls Nation delegate. Goff had noticed her leadership skills and encouraged Smith's political development with invitations back to Girls State as a staff member in the early 1960s. The two women traveled to Europe later in 1966. When Smith was sworn in on the Court of Appeals in 1991 Goff attended. Smith's mother commented to Frances: "You ought to be here. You're the one that got her into all of this!" Smith became a strong advocate for racial justice while a student at the University of Texas at Austin. As a college student, Smith spent much of her time working with the YWCA's race relations conference. Smith recalled the

Registration of an unidentified African American Citizen at Girls State in 1964; in the background are Brownie Moore, Corliss Beasley, Kay Cude, two unidentified women, Martha Toles, and an unidentified Citizen; at the registration table is Nedra Ogle of the American Legion Auxiliary. *CN 08979. Courtesy Frances Goff Papers, Center for American History, University of Texas at Austin.*

events surrounding the vote on integrating the program. Dorothy Cooper was president of the ALA at the time. With her friend Maurine Martin ensconced as chair of the Auxiliary's Girls State Committee, Frances "insisted on the vote [for integration] being taken on a voice vote, and had all of us in the room visiting, and we all voted and it passed, and that's the only way Girls State got integrated."

The year 1964 proved momentous for civil rights advances. Not only did Congress pass at Lyndon Johnson's behest a major Civil Rights Act but also individual groups and organizations made steps toward a more pluralistic society. Indeed, Girls State was no exception because under Frances's leadership the ALA program in Texas broke the color line that year. Among the first black Citizens at Girls State, Jackie Howard of Texarkana was elected attorney general in 1964 on the Federalist Party ticket. She returned as a staff member in 1965. Even though the selection procedure varied from community to

F. Mead Griffin swears in Jackie Howard as the 1964 Attorney General, the first African American elected to an office at Girls State. Behind Howard is Texas Attorney General Waggoner Carr. *CN 08980. Courtesy Frances Goff Papers, Center for American History, University of Texas at Austin.*

community, the high schools played an important role in the process of sending young black women to Austin for Girls State. The majority of Texas high schools were segregated in 1964 as were the ALA units. After gaining approval for inviting African American Citizens to Girls State, Frances coordinated with the black units to ensure a smooth transition. These units worked through the black high schools and twelve or so of the 402 Citizens that year were African American.

Frances requested that staff and counselors with the program treat the black Citizens with dignity and respect. Arliss Treybig, a Citizen from 1952, remembered that another un-named staff member told Frances: "This is going to be hard for me. . . . I'm going to do the best I can. It's going to be hard for me. If I do anything wrong, you tell me." In the first year of integration, ALA units statewide asked prospective Citizens how they felt about having an African American roommate. When parents in the mid 1960s complained, the staff told them they could take their daughters home.

As part of her plans for integrating Girls State, Frances invited Mary Mead, a Citizen and governor in 1954, to give the keynote address at Girls State in 1964. Mead had joined a convent and became Sister Mary Bernadette of the Order of Dominican Sisters of the Sacred Heart Dominican in Houston. Goff

Sister Mary Bernadette with Frances Goff, 1964. *CN 08983. Courtesy Frances Goff Papers, Center for American History, University of Texas at Austin.*

described her speech as the "most inspirational address" she had ever heard. Furthermore, Goff noted that Sister Mary Bernadette's speech "set the spirit of brotherhood and oneness which prevailed throughout a most successful first integrated Girls State Session." On June 19, 1964, a writer for *The Bluebonnet* noted that Sister Mary Bernadette "spoke with more power and significance than all of" the Citizens combined.

The former governor of Girls State challenged her audience to retain spiritual values: "There's a contradiction, isn't there, in the glamour of a city that has beautiful glass and marble buildings and terrible crime, social disorders within it? There's a vast discrepancy here. You notice this, and this is one of the things that bring a conflict into your life. The very great difference between what is set up as great and what you know to exist." Sister Mary Bernadette exhorted the Citizens to approach their lives with human compassion for others and never to put off for someone else what they themselves could accomplish.

For the first integrated year of Girls State, Goff invited Luci Johnson, the daughter of President Lyndon B. Johnson and Lady Bird Johnson, to be a Citizen. In a March 4, 1964, letter preserved in the White House Social Files, Goff proposed to the president's younger daughter that "It is sincerely hoped that you will be interested in our endeavors and can accept our invitation for this year. I shall look forward to hearing from you and if it is possible for you to attend, additional information will be transmitted." The Austin Democratic congressman, Jake Pickle, endorsed the program and suggested Luci accept the invitation. He wrote to Lady Bird Johnson on April 16, 1964, that "Frances Goff does a tremendously good job, and I know that Luci would enjoy the occasion and would make a tremendous contribution to those girls if she could go." Nevertheless, Luci eventually declined the invitation because of a summer job.

Part of the integration process involved bringing in a rising politician, who happened to be female and African American, as a speaker one year after the inclusion of minorities as Citizens. That speaker, the first African American ever at Girls State, was Barbara Jordan. The year was 1965. Although Frances had never met Barbara Jordan, she knew the emerging politician by reputation. Former Citizens encouraged Frances along these lines. Bea Ann Smith's work with the YWCA's race relations conference introduced her to Barbara Jordan. Smith then pushed for her invitation to speak at Girls State.

Rubyrae described the scene when Jordan proceeded to the stage on her first visit to Girls State: "None of the girls or anybody knew that Barbara Jordan was black, just that she was on the program. But, when she came down the aisle and she was presented and the girls first realized it and you look at the expressions on their faces, it tells volumes about where we were in integration at that time. . . . Of course she gave a wonderful speech."

Dale Simons reflected that "you could just hear it, and they listened to every word she said, and got a standing ovation, you would not believe the enthusiasm." Marsha Grissom remembered that "when she came walking

Bea Ann Smith escorts Barbara Jordan at Girls State in 1965. *CN 08907. Courtesy Texas Bluebonnet Girls State, Center for American History, University of Texas at Austin.*

down the aisle to come in, it was like you could see mouths drop. It was like, wait a minute. When she got to the stage and she opened her mouth, you

Barbara Jordan with Frances Goff, 1968. *CN 08978. Courtesy Frances Goff Papers, Center for American History, University of Texas at Austin.*

could have heard a pin on that hot gym floor."

Barbara Jordan, the first African American to be an administrative assistant to the County Judge of Harris County, addressed the Citizens on June 23, 1965, on the theme of the dignity of man. Her speech, entitled "No Time to Dream," argued that too many politicians were "profit motivated" instead of "service motivated." In a return visit in 1966, Jordan told a reporter for *The Bluebonnet* on June 18, 1966, that her membership in the Liberal Democratic Coalition resulted because "there are proposals and programs that the liberals of this state have always been interested in. I'm just going to step up and follow suit on industrial safety, effective air and water pollution, and minimum wage—all of the traditional programs we've always been concerned about. I think we need a sound and resolute voice pushing these things." Jordan returned to Girls State each summer through the early 1970s until her congressional duties became too burdensome because of her involvement in the Watergate hearings.

When asked about Girls State integration and the use of Barbara Jordan to smooth that process, Pat Mathis described Frances as "a very elaborately constructed moralist, and she has all sorts of rules, dos, don'ts and all that sort of stuff. I don't think she would just embrace Barbara Jordan because it was the fashion of the day. I think she was truly captured by her magnetism. Frances saw that this was a politically feasible thing to do."

Jordan's speech was a success; it showed the intelligence and ability of one very talented African American woman. Arliss Treybig remembered Jordan's skill at dealing with questions about blacks in America. Jordan declared, "Blacks will always be a visible minority. Many of you in other cultures you can begin to blend over the years, but we never will."

During this period Brownie Moore ceased her involvement with Girls State and ended what had become a very important friendship with Goff. Some sort of rupture occurred between the two women, yet thirty years after the fact the exact nature of the dispute remains mysterious. Frances Goff gave her friendship to many people, but when a friend's actions did not comport with her high standards she could be very severe in her reaction. Moore's performance had done something to convince Frances that her onetime friend was not reliable and trustworthy, and she had no further official dealings with Moore.

In fact, Brownie Moore's last year as assistant to the director was 1965. Her last year on the Girls State Committee was 1966. On June 22, 1966, *The Bluebonnet* wrote that "a familiar face is missing from Girls State this year— that of a former Citizen, Junior Counselor, Senior Counselor, assistant director and now member of the Texas Girls State Committee of the ALA." However,

Frances Goff with George Bush and Virginia Bailey in the background at Girls State in the late 1960s. The photo is inscribed "With High Regards and Warm Best Wishes, George Bush." *CN 08958. Courtesy Frances Goff Papers, Center for American History, University of Texas at Austin.*

Moore remained active in local Democratic Party politics and she assisted her husband in his campaign for district judge.

Despite her convictions about integration, Frances's politics retained a conservative bent into the 1960s. It was during the 1960s that Frances became close with a rising Texas Republican, George Bush. Despite the comparatively weak position of the Texas Republicans in the 1960s, party activists split their loyalties between two power bases. John Tower, the senior Senator from Texas, maintained a stronghold on West Texas Republicanism while Bush and Paul Eggers, an unsuccessful Republican candidate for governor of Texas in 1968 and 1970, dominated the Houston GOP. Despite Tower's greater name recognition, Goff gravitated toward Bush because, as Anne Hodges Morgan, who joined Senator Tower's legislative staff in 1963, explained, "she knew Bush. Frances is loyal to her friends." George Bush also spoke during these years at Girls State. In the late 1960s and early 1970s, Eggers was a regular speaker at Girls State.

High-profile speakers were not selected solely from the ranks of the GOP. Frances's ability to get quality people on the program reached all the way to

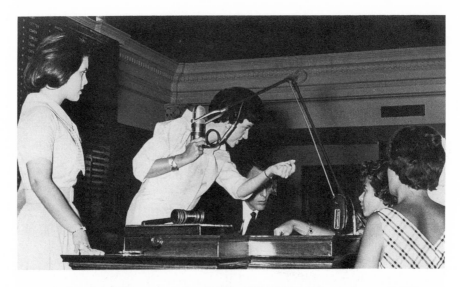

Anne Hodges at Girls State in the late 1960s. *CN 08995. Courtesy Frances Goff Papers, Center for American History, University of Texas at Austin.*

the White House in the late 1960s. Despite her life-long dislike for Lyndon B. Johnson, Goff convinced Lady Bird Johnson to attend Girls State in 1967. Along with her media entourage, Mrs. Johnson spent an hour with the Girls State officials and spoke to the Citizens in what probably was the first appearance of a First Lady at a Girls State event anywhere in the nation. In a letter that has been preserved in the White House Social Files of the LBJ Library, Goff wrote to Mrs. Johnson on July 26 of her "hope [that] the excitement and enthusiasm of our Citizens was as rewarding to you as your appearance was to them. . . . Please know this was the highlight of the 1967 Girls State session and a never to be forgotten experience for all who were present." The 1967 session also saw the first meeting of officials from the Austin city government and the Travis County government with the Citizens.

Inviting former Citizens who had done well in the world back as speakers became increasingly possible in the 1960s as Goff's protégés built their own careers. On June 19, 1968, Anne Hodges delivered a powerful speech to the Citizens of Girls State that has since been preserved in Goff's papers. Hodges made a pessimistic assessment of the health of the nation in the wake of the recent wave of rioting. "Youth power has become a new phrase in our vocabulary and it truly is a reality. My question to you is what kind of youth power are you going to make it. Will you burn buildings out of hatred, dis-

Former President Lyndon B. Johnson and Lady Bird Johnson escorted to the podium by Ester Chavez, 1969. *CN 08973. Courtesy Frances Goff Papers, Center for American History, University of Texas at Austin.*

satisfaction and frustration, or will you have the energy and the stamina to choose the more difficult path of constructive reform?" Hodges stressed the importance of ballots and political parties as weapons for change. Indeed, the speech—advocating reasoned political actions through the proper channels— and the speaker—a young woman who had herself been a Citizen of Girls State—reveal much about Frances's own political evolution in the tumultuous 1960s.

At the end of the 1969 session Lyndon and Lady Bird Johnson made a "surprise" visit to the Girls State closing ceremony. President Johnson spoke about "The Responsibility of Women in the American Government and Politics." At the conclusion of the session Goff thanked the Johnsons for their participation and invited them back for future programs. In 1970, however, Johnson declined and noted on a June 25 memo in his papers that "I'm getting too involved."

Former President Johnson would be the last prominent speaker to address Girls State Citizens in their traditional headquarters of Austin. By the end of the 1970s, Girls State faced another moment of decision as an organization.

Should they move away from Austin to expanded quarters elsewhere? The decisions that Frances Goff made about that issue would take the Girls State program into the modern phase of its existence.

Chapter 9

Wider Horizons in the 1970s

The late 1960s and the early 1970s were years of flux for Girls State. A major ingredient in the success of Girls State resulted from the closed, tight-knit community Frances Goff created for the duration of the session. Yet these conditions proved more difficult to maintain by the late 1960s. During this time Frances had to search out a more suitable home for Girls State. A rising population in the city of Austin and at the University of Texas presented Frances with a serious challenge for maintaining the disciplined atmosphere of Girls State. To keep the young women focused on the study of government, Frances tolerated no outside distractions. Yet the dynamics of the state's capital no longer seemed welcoming. Austin had grown to a city of 250,000 residents with 27,000 students at the University of Texas. The very characteristics that had made Austin the ideal community to host Girls State in the late 1940s were gone by the late 1960s.

In the immediate postwar years Austin had been a sleepy community centered on the state government and the university making it the perfect city to host Girls State. When the program moved from Waco to Austin in 1947, the capital city had a population of 150,000 with 17,000 students at the University of Texas. From 1947 through 1949, Girls State was held at the Texas School for the Blind. However, the American Legion Auxiliary relocated temporarily to the Texas School for the Deaf for the years 1950–1954. Girls State went back to the School for the Blind in 1955 where it stayed until 1968. That year the ALA began having Girls State at St. Edward's University because the School for the Blind started holding summer classes. St. Edward's University, a Catholic liberal arts school located in South Austin, had been a male-only institution until 1966 when it admitted its first female students.

Frances approached the move to St. Edward's with "great faith and flexibility" and cautioned others to do the same according to a memorandum that she wrote to the ALA Department president, secretary, and Girls State Committee on March 27, 1968. Planning for the first year at St. Edward's presented numerous challenges. Higher costs for food and housing caused the budget for 1968 to increase by $10,000 from the previous year. The arrangement of the dormitories on campus proved problematic to the placement of the mythical cities and counties within Girls State. Frances hoped that there would be continuity in the staff and counselor positions unlike the previous year when there had been a "grand exodus at the last minute." Frances spoke of her excitement over the impending arrival of Grace Baldwin, her long-time friend, from Okinawa. Baldwin returned to Houston for a conference of elementary school principals. "It was January two years ago that she was last home so I feel sure that work on Girls State will be at a standstill until her departure."

Frances overcame these difficulties and Girls State enjoyed two productive years at St. Edward's. The university gained positive public relations and increased visibility during the years Girls State used their facilities. Some of the Citizens found the campus so appealing that they returned for their undergraduate studies. Citizens increasingly reflected the turbulent times of the late 1960s. In 1968, the young women adopted the theme of "born free" for their scrapbook. However, the tenure of Girls State at St. Edward's University proved short-lived. By 1970, Frances was searching for a new home for the program.

Finding suitable arrangements for the location of the 1970 session proved difficult. Officials with St. Edward's University seemed unwilling to commit to hosting the annual event. Nevertheless, these individuals insisted that if the Girls State program returned to their campus then the fee per girl per day should increase from $4.50 to $6.50. As a result of the uncertainty at St. Edward's, Frances toured the women's portion of the Jester Center dormitory at the University of Texas at Austin on October 4, 1969. UT officials promised a rate of $5.50 a day for each person. Later that day, Frances took that price to the St. Edward's people who then agreed to meet that price and indicated facilities on campus should be available. Based on these findings, Frances and the Girls State Committee decided to raise the fee for each girl to $75.

At the end of October 1969, Goff learned from the people at St. Edward's that the university had closed their facilities to groups with over 100 participants. With Girls State scheduled to convene in fewer than eight months,

Frances began calling schools in the Austin and South Texas area: Southwestern University in Georgetown; Trinity University, St. Mary's University, and Incarnate Word University all in San Antonio; and Texas Lutheran College in Seguin. Because of prior commitments on the part of the Georgetown and San Antonio institutions, Texas Lutheran College became the only option other than the University of Texas. Frances and some of the members of the staff visited the Seguin campus on Saturday, November 22, 1969.

A city of 15,000 residents in 1969, Seguin was located about forty miles east of San Antonio and about fifty-five miles south of Austin. The town had grown during the 1950s and 1960s and promised to be an ideal location for Girls State. Seguin boasted around thirty industrial firms by the early 1970s when Frances relocated Girls State out of Austin. Texas Lutheran College dated its existence to 1891. By the early 1970s, the 101-acre campus served approximately 1,000 students and had ample facilities to house the Girls State program each summer. In fact, dormitory space made it possible for Frances to accommodate a larger number of Citizens each year. Registration increased from the 400 Citizens accepted each year in the 1960s to almost 600 by the early 1990s.

In a letter dated December 10, 1969, Frances told the members of the Girls State Committee that "I cannot tell you how enthusiastically we were received in Seguin and while there are some things not desirable, others are and I do feel we made the right move in relocating the session rather than having it at the University." Rubyrae Phillips agreed that Texas Lutheran College seemed very receptive to the Girls State Program. "They looked upon it as a real boon to the college." Furthermore, Rubyrae recalled that "Frances felt very comfortable working with that staff and she was very impressed with the level of academia with the people there." Seguin and Texas Lutheran College promised other more tangible benefits in the form of lower costs which made possible limiting the registration fee to $70 per girl.

The citizens of Seguin welcomed their new two-week summer residents. Seguin newspapers celebrated the arrival of the 500 Citizens of Girls State in June 1970. For the first time since 1947, the American Legion Auxiliary located the Girls State program outside of Austin. In its June 18 edition, the Seguin *Gazette* proclaimed: "The Gazette in behalf of its readers extends a big 'Welcome to Seguin' to our 500 guests. . . . You've done Seguin great honor in selecting this community to conduct your program this year. . . . Rest assured that we of Seguin will work diligently for your return here in each succeeding year." Girls State also seemed pleased with its new home.

George Bush with unidentified Citizens, 1970. *CN 08977. Courtesy Frances Goff Papers, Center for American History, University of Texas at Austin.*

The article on the move to Seguin explained how happy the staff was with its new home. The local paper revealed that area printers were more willing to work on the production of the Girls State newspaper, *The Bluebonnet,* than were Austin printers. And the local newspapers suggested that the facilities at Texas Lutheran College were better suited to handle the burgeoning Girls State program. These papers printed the names of city residents who had previously been Citizens of Girls State.

Girls State lived up to the ballyhoo that year. The paper promised significant speakers, many of whom were Frances's friends and political associates. Indeed, the 1970 program included several prominent people, among whom

Lloyd Bentsen with Frances Goff. *CN 08971. Courtesy Frances Goff Papers, Center for American History, University of Texas at Austin.*

were Lloyd Bentsen and George Bush, the Democratic and Republican nominees for the U.S. Senate, Paul Eggers, Republican candidate for governor, Preston Smith, the incumbent Democratic governor, Barbara Jordan, still a member of the state senate, and numerous other dignitaries.

That year the Citizens of City G welcomed George Bush, the future president, to their gathering. They made Bush an honorary gherkin pickle, and the incumbent Republican congressman promised, according to the Seguin *Enterprise* on June 25, to always "be a sweet pickle." In his speech, Bush challenged the young women "to change things within the framework of the system." Bush then agreed with sentiment popular among America's youth that an early end to the Vietnam War was necessary. "There is no question about it. We have to get out of Vietnam and whip the question that is dividing the country."

Lloyd Bentsen, Bush's Democratic opponent and the eventual victor in their Senate race, told the Citizens that "this nation is frustrated. It is frustrated in the Vietnam War, the multitude of social problems at home. It is frustrated by the threat of anarchy on one extreme and the threat of dictatorship on the other extreme. . . . Let's guard our priceless heritage . . . let's perfect our democracy. . . . Young people like you hold the key."

Long-time Seguin resident and Democratic Party activist Hilda Weinert journeyed with the Citizens into Austin for their inauguration ceremonies. According to the June 25 Seguin *Gazette*, she then gave an impromptu speech on the importance of political activity. "Choose a party to be affiliated with. Love your party. And WORK for your party." Weinert made a strong impact on the Citizens, who appreciated her candor.

An episode from the 1970 Girls Nation symbolized another major problem Frances handled. With her leadership of Bluebonnet Girls State in Texas firmly entrenched, Frances turned her attention to Girls Nation in what eventually proved an unsuccessful effort to broaden the opportunities for young Texas women to learn about national government. In 1970, Tanya Starnes, one of the two Texas delegates, was selected vice president at Girls Nation. However, her election was controversial and resulted in raising Frances's frustration level with the National program. Both Starnes and the other Texas Delegate, Steffi Sandler, were in the Federalist Party at Girls Nation, and both had ambitions for political office. Sandler ran for the presidency of Girls Nation that year.

After Starnes received the nomination for the vice presidency in the party conventions, staff members at Girls Nation announced a last minute decision that both representatives from the same state could not be candidates for the top two offices. At the time of the announcement, Sandler had already made her speech to the party convention. Frances learned of the situation when she received a late night phone call from Starnes. She quickly phoned her contacts in Washington to protest the midstream changes in the rules. Goff pointed out that the Girls Nation president and vice president in 1968 had both been from Idaho.

In an August 17, 1970, letter to Mrs. T. G. Chilton, the chair of the National Girls State Committee, Frances complained that "this confused process of policy making during the election of nominees caused adverse reaction of these young ladies to your program. The Texas delegates had recently experienced a highly organized and structured program at their Girls State; hence, they had not anticipated any complications of this nature." Frances felt that she deserved some sort of explanation of the procedures for

Senior Counselors from 1962. Back row, left to right: Margaret Boerner, Lucy Puryear Yoder, Mary Flynt, Marsha Barnett, Jewell Schmidt. Front row, left to right: Marilyn Hahn, Arliss Treybig, Mary Ellen Trahan. *CN 08965. Courtesy Texas Bluebonnet Girls State, Center for American History, University of Texas at Austin.*

that year. "I deeply resent no communication as it would appear Texas is at least due a reply to the inquiry." While no response exists within Goff's papers, these developments led her to devise an alternative to Girls Nation.

By the early 1970s, Frances pushed for an internship program because she had grown frustrated with the Girls Nation program. She wanted some sort of program that would instruct young Texas women about the workings of their national government. Since Girls Nation seemed more like a vacation, Frances proposed a week-long internship for a dozen or so Bluebonnet Girls State Citizens. Selections would be made at the end of the ten-day Girls State session and the internship would begin in July.

According to Arliss Treybig, Frances believed that Girls Nation lacked any serious educational component and had evolved into a "little trip to Washington, more a little social thing." Girls Nation delegates from the 1950s and 1960s agreed. Mary Ellen Trahan, a 1958 Citizen and Girls Nation delegate, told a reporter for the June 14, 1969, *Bluebonnet* that "there was not enough time devoted to the legislature." Trahan's successor

Jo Hudson, Mary Ellen Trahan, Frances Goff, 1985. *CN 08960. Courtesy Frances Goff Papers, Center for American History, University of Texas at Austin.*

from 1968, Beverly Fecel, agreed: "Debate and legislation at Girls Nation were not as interesting as at Girls State."

Senator Bentsen with interns in 1974. First row, left to right: Nora Faye Housley, Katherine Karp, Connie Grusendorf. Second row, left to right: Jody Berryman, Senator Bentsen, Mikie Collier, Beth Ryan. Third row, left to right: Katie Meyer, Katherine Mitchell, Mary Ann Wissel, Rhonda Graff, Mary Williams, Collyn Peddie. Fourth row, left to right: Counselors for the trip were Chris Burlingame, Edie Richardson, and Mary Ellen Trahan. *CN 08940. Courtesy Texas Bluebonnet Girls State, Center for American History, University of Texas at Austin.*

Frances wanted to exert her influence over the Girls Nation program, but that proved impossible. Goff believed that the cap of two on how many young women could go on to Girls Nation was too restrictive. She hoped that time in Washington, D.C., would benefit more people and improve the connections between the Girls State network and the outside political community. The National ALA, though, permitted an almost yearly rotation of staff and resisted the reform efforts Frances had in mind. Lloyd Bentsen, now Democratic Senator from Texas, proved willing to help Frances around her dilemma.

In 1972, Goff worked with Bentsen and established an Internship Program for twelve Girls State Citizens. The Girls State Committee and the ALA

Connie Grusendorf with Governor Dolph Briscoe. *CN 08947. Courtesy Texas Bluebonnet Girls State, Center for American History, University of Texas at Austin.*

expressed their approval of the plan, which would send the girls to Washington along with chaperones for five or six days. Senator Bentsen helped with the costs of housing and expenses while the ALA Girls State Committee covered the transportation expenses. The first interns departed on July 8, 1973. Bentsen and his office staff compiled impressive itineraries for the young women. They visited with members of Congress, the executive branch, and employees at the Supreme Court, as well as taking in the sites of the Smithsonian and a production at the National Theater. The senator also provided the interns with biographical material on the individuals the interns would meet during their stay.

Occasionally the new program presented logistical challenges. In 1973 and again in 1975, Frances had to make special travel arrangements for the two Girls Nation delegates because they were scheduled to serve in the Bentsen Internship Program immediately before Girls Nation. When these situations arose, Frances negotiated with the National American Legion Auxiliary to cover the costs of Girls Nation and ensure that the young women in question could take part in both activities.

The Internship Program continued in 1974. The interns spent five days in the nation's capital meeting with individuals from all branches of the federal government, including Democratic Cong. Jim Wright of Fort Worth; Casper Weinberger, the secretary of Health, Education, and Welfare in the Richard Nixon administration; Sen. Henry Jackson of Washington; Sen. Robert Byrd of West Virginia, Sen. John Tower of Texas; and Sen. Lowell Weicker of Connecticut. They also met with influential newspaper publisher Katherine Graham of the *Washington Post*.

Connie Gruesendorf Bridges was among the young women who went to Washington, D.C., as an intern in 1974. She was there during the tumultuous days of Watergate. On July 9, 1974, the *Washington Post* carried a photograph of Leon Jaworski, the Watergate special prosecutor, entering the Supreme Court for oral arguments and Connie Gruesendorf was one of the people in the background. Mary Ellen Trahan accompanied the group as a chaperone. Trahan wrote to the interns after their return home "to remind you of the trip and give you an opportunity to think back again of the wonderful things that happened while we were in D.C. I know you've thought back over the fully-packed week we spent in Washington with much sentiment and 'wunnerful' memories. . . . I'm sure it will be an asset to you throughout your senior year and for that matter, your lifetime, for you were there when history was being made."

Connie, who went on to play an important role as counselor and staff member in the Girls State program, caught Frances's eye. Elected governor of Girls State in 1974, she came back as a staff member in 1975. On June 26, 1975, Frances wrote to her: "Prior to and upon your departure from Girls State I tried to let you know just how much your efforts toward the 1975 session were appreciated. Saying 'thank you' for a job well done is most difficult but please know how deeply I feel toward your devotion and loyalty to our program."

Frances lobbied successfully for continuing the Internship Program in 1975. According to a report that the chaperones for the Bentsen Internship program made to Frances and the Girls State staff, the Texas participants enjoyed a rewarding week of activities that year. They met with Robert Strauss, then the chair of the Democratic National Committee, and learned about the reforms currently underway in Democratic Party policy toward delegate selection for the conventions. Hubert Humphrey, a senator from Minnesota, endorsed a system of regional presidential primaries instead of the longer, drawn-out process currently employed. The Senate Majority Leader Mike Mansfield spoke favorably about the changes to the seniority system in Congress. From other members of the Senate the young women learned of the financial burden that resulted from effective constituent service; the procurement of wedding, birth, and graduation announcements was just one example. Cong. Lindy Boggs of Louisiana made a favorable impression on the young women. Boggs had lost her husband, Hale, to a plane crash in Alaska in 1973. As a result she took over his seat in Congress. The chaperones declared "she is our picture of the ideal woman. . . . She is a most capable person in her own right and has since been re-elected to the House on her own merit. Quite a lady!" Bentsen devoted an hour and a half from his schedule to visiting with the girls. The chaperones reported that "he really seemed to enjoy the girls and was interested in their impressions of Washington. We enjoyed the relaxed atmosphere of our time with Senator Bentsen and the girls especially appreciated being his special group."

Despite praise from some individuals within the ALA, Frances's Internship Program encountered opposition and its renewal faced a stiff challenge in 1975. Eleanor McCray, the secretary-treasurer of the Texas ALA, wrote to Frances on January 21, 1975, about the budget for the coming session of Girls State. Although she had questions about the distribution of funds, McCray made clear that "I know the Girls State Program will do well. I wish all my problems and worries were as small as the ones I have experienced over this Program . . . thanks to you and the wonderful girls you have working with you." While the year began on a positive note, problems marked the end of 1975 for Frances and Girls State.

At the September 27, 1975, meeting of the Girls State Committee, Frances reported her analysis of her meeting the previous day with the Finance Committee over funding for Girls State. At issue was funding for the Bentsen Internship Program. During that committee meeting, members questioned the payment of transportation expenses for the Bentsen Interns. Finance Committee members argued that the expenditures should never have been made because the American Legion convention had not voted its approval. Frances disputed this claim, arguing that the Executive Committee had authorized the Internship Program in the fall of 1972. Furthermore, she stressed that the matter had never gone to the full convention.

A three-member majority of the Finance Committee wrote a report declaring that the Girls State funds from the American Legion Auxiliary should only be spent for the Girls State Program proper. A minority of the Finance Committee recommended the continuation of the Internship Program. Finance Committee members also questioned the insurance carried for Girls State and its coverage of the Interns. Frances promised that she would investigate these points.

Frances informed the Finance Committee that she would address the issues of the Internship program at the Bi-Centennial Boys–Girls State and Nation Program in Indianapolis in early October. She reported that the states would be asked to create internship programs similar to the Bentsen Internship Program for Bluebonnet Girls State at this meeting. Frances also indicated that she would discuss the matter of insurance coverage with the S. S. Van Dyke Company, the carrier of the Girls State policy, at the Indianapolis meeting. Frances proposed that the Finance Committee report opposing the internship program be tabled pending the results of her trip to Indianapolis.

Frances also quarreled with the Finance Committee that year over the fee for Girls State. The Finance Committee wanted a slight reduction in the amount charged the ALA members for the Girls State program. Frances asserted that, with the final amount of the registration fee for the Girls State program still undetermined because of the lack of a final food budget, reducing the fee might prove a wrong move if the committee later came back and asked for the larger amount.

In the middle of November, Mary Helen Rodriguez, the department president, wrote to Goff and informed her that the Executive Committee had voted by a margin of 29–2 on October 21 "that Bluebonnet Girls State registration fees be used only for the American Legion Auxiliary Girls State

Session in Texas and for Girls Nation." This decision effectively killed the Internship Program. The vote also approved a reduced budget for Girls State. Rodriguez asked Goff if the fee charged each local ALA unit for registration of the Citizens could be reduced. Rodriguez made the request because "there is such a nice balance in the 1975 Girls State Budget" and because "Girls State is financially secure in that for the past few years a balance from that Fund has been placed in a Savings Account."

Rodriguez explained that membership had fallen off by 5,000 names from the 18,000 people who paid dues in 1974. She declared: "Frances, the Units are hard-pressed for membership—money to finance projects—Rehabilitation Programs within their own communities—then the increase in dues this past year has not helped. . . . There are too many ladies with a fixed-income which makes it difficult to keep them on the membership rolls." Despite acknowledging the scholastic accomplishments of Girls State, Rodriguez argued the program simply cost too much money.

Rodriguez questioned Goff's financial management of Girls State. She asked whether the money-making operation of the Girls State store honored the non-profit status of the program. Rodriguez complained: "A check for a nice amount was sent to the Department Headquarters as profit from this past Session and this could be a cause for problems with the Office of the Comptroller. . . . We certainly do not want to jeopardize the entire organization by making a profit and not reporting same." Rodriguez asked Goff for an explanation but assured "there is nothing 'personal' in this business matter—as it is strictly business and am sure you realize this. We feel that the Girls State Committee is like any other committee and *any* consideration by the Girls State Committee should be *correct* and *voted upon by the entire Body* so that ALL will know just where the money is being used." Rodriguez indicated the Girls State Committee would not tolerate actions that led to problems with the state comptroller. "This could be serious, and we wish to hear from you and your intentions about this for the coming session."

Goff responded to Rodriguez one month later and expressed her anger about the cancellation of the Internship Program, which she had hoped would play a key role in the nation's bicentennial celebration the following year. Goff criticized the lack of knowledge which the Finance Committee members had about Girls State. She noted only one person on that important committee had any appreciation or experience with Girls State. "I am sorry that the Finance Committee . . . saw fit to undertake the destruction of one of the finest programs ever established for our outstanding girls of each session," Frances protested. Furthermore Goff stressed that the Executive

Committee had approved the Internship Program in 1972 and no amount of denial on the part of the program's opponents would prove otherwise.

Goff insisted that the Internship Program had been conducted publicly, despite the contrary assertions Rodriguez and others had made. Goff reminded her adversary of the 1973 ALA convention in San Antonio where a detailed report on the first Girls State Internship Program had been made. Goff reserved her harshest criticisms for the way that the Finance Committee conducted its vote without advising her of its intentions. "I am also sorry that you and the Finance Committee did not at least have the courtesy to advise me that you were going to send this out for a vote when you did." After all, Goff reminded Rodriguez, the matter of the internships had been tabled earlier that fall depending the outcome of her trip to the national ALA convention in October where she was to investigate plans for a national internship program and insurance coverage for the existing Bentsen Internship Program. When the vote was taken Goff had received none of the answers she had promised the committee. "Consequently I was surprised and disturbed that this was done without any notification to me."

Goff also criticized plans to reduce the registration fee. "You will recall I stated when I met with the Finance Committee that our cost at Texas Lutheran was not firm as there was still negotiation relative to the food cost with their catering company to be made after the first of the year." Goff explained the necessity of maintaining "a secure balance in the Girls State fund for unexpected emergencies." Goff also defended the Girls State certificates of deposit as part of a plan to produce a color sound film of Girls State for public relations purposes. She indicated such a film would have immeasurable value for local units.

Goff asserted that "one of the reasons we have been able to save money is that I have begged, borrowed, and scrounged from agencies and individuals to make contributions, monetarily and otherwise, to the program." For example, Goff explained her own personal contribution to the printing expenses Girls State incurred. She then warned that such arrangements might end in the near future, causing a dramatic increase in Girls State costs. Goff then destroyed Rodriguez's argument that increasing costs would ruin Girls State by noting other community organizations sponsored the costs of over half of all Citizens. Goff also noted that Girls State had turned prospective Citizens away for lack of space, so she indicated the fees must not be that significant a problem. Goff then returned to the same arguments she had made to the ALA earlier that fall about reducing registration fees. "With the increased cost of everything, I feel it psychologically bad to reduce the fee this year and then have to raise it considerably next year and I feel certain this would be true because of the increase in housing and food at Texas Lutheran College."

Goff also quickly dispatched Rodriguez's criticisms of the Girls State store. She explained that as an educational organization, Girls State was exempt from collecting taxes. Neither were the profits immense. For example, two years later the store managed a net profit of $2,023.83. Goff assured there was never an attempt to hide Girls State expenditures. "Many years ago we started going before the Finance Committee to review our budget. . . . This was not mandatory at that time but I think I have been doing this for the last 15 years or more as a matter of courtesy and information." Then Goff declared: "If your statement is an implication of misuse of funds, it is resented. I do not think the members of the Auxiliary realize how much time and effort is put forth on this program. It does not just run itself. . . . Through these [volunteer] efforts we have reached a highly structured educational program. It would be regrettable to see the program deteriorate at this time." Notwithstanding Goff's vigorous rebuttal, the Bentsen Internship Program died in the mid-1970s.

Despite the ALA's victory over the Internship Program, Frances retained funding for a Girls State film. In 1977, Goff arranged for the production of a thirty-minute film about Girls State. The governor from 1976, Kappy Allen, served as the narrator for the film. Private donations and savings from the Girls State budget over the past five years paid for the film. Mary and Kenneth E. Bentsen, the latter a Houston architect and brother of Lloyd Bentsen, donated $250 to the filming of 1977 session. John S. Dunn Sr., a Houston philanthropist concerned primarily with health-care issues and cancer treatment, contributed $1,000 for the film account, as did the Strake Foundation, a Houston-based trust established in 1952 with an emphasis on programs for youth. Republicans and Democrats had underwritten this tribute to the work of Girls State.

By the mid-1970s, Girls State had a clear identity of what it was about: a program dedicated to highlighting female leadership potential. In 1975, Citizens passed a resolution abandoning the term "Girls Stater" because the young women believed it had derogatory undertones. But Girls State also became more relaxed with the use of former Citizens as speakers. For example, in 1977 four of the five speakers were former Girls State Citizens: Bea Ann Smith, an attorney and Citizen from 1960; Martha Smiley, an attorney and Citizen from 1963; Carole Keeton McClellan (Rylander after 1983), the Austin mayor and a Citizen from 1956; and Sharon Bintliff, a doctor and

Connie Grusendorf with other Citizens and cake. *CN 08948. Courtesy Texas Bluebonnet Girls State, Center for American History, University of Texas at Austin.*

Citizen from 1952. The other speaker was LBJ School of Public Affairs Dean Elspeth Rostow. Gone were the days of dressing in their Sunday best for the assemblies. Instead Frances permitted the Citizens to wear shorts and be more casual. Arliss Treybig observed that Frances had "mellowed." Treybig also remembered that it was during this time that Frances expanded the educational component of the program. She seemed more willing to experiment with additional court cases and urban problems for the girls to consider.

Indeed, Frances relied on past Citizens to play a strong role in the Girls State programs. Carole Keeton McClellan graduated from the University of Texas at Austin in 1961 and became active with the Austin school board in the early 1970s. She served as Austin mayor from 1977 to 1983, and would later be elected to the Texas Railroad Commission in 1994. In a speech reported in *The Bluebonnet* on June 26, 1979, McClellan told the Citizens in 1979 that they should speak out on the issues. "And there's nothing unladylike about that. . . . We must assert ourselves in the causes of human well-being and human decency. You have to have the courage to speak out on convictions and to draw moral lines between right and wrong."

Carole Keeton McClellan, 1977. *CN 08910. Courtesy Texas Bluebonnet Girls State, Center for American History, University of Texas at Austin.*

By the end of the 1970s, the relationship with Texas Lutheran College experienced growing pains as it matured into genuine partnership. In a rare moment of frustration with her various public responsibilities, Frances wrote to Anne Morgan on March 10, 1978: "wish I could join you to be free of meetings and fools and watch the soaps on TV." Frances more often looked at the Texas Lutheran College partnership as beneficial to the Girls State program. Frances wrote to Theos Morck, a Seguin-area businessman, on July 3,

1979, and declared that "we had a good session of Girls State but it just does-n't seem to be the same as it was when we started, however, the new adminis-tration is beginning to understand that we really are not 'looney' in some of our requests." Frances then observed that "this year marked the 10th year we have been at Texas Lutheran College and believe me, it seems like only yester-day that we made the original trip to talk to you and Dr. [Joe E.] Menn."

Frances Goff took Girls State to greater heights in the 1970s. She found a new home for the program that proved ideal for retaining the close-knit feel of the Girls State community even as society became more and more splintered. Furthermore, Frances never lost her sense of how Girls State should function. For a brief time, she succeeded in bringing her vision of government educa-tion to the national level. The ultimate failure of the Bentsen Internship Program proved the only major defeat for Frances in her travails with the ALA. Despite this setback, Frances retained a strong working partnership with the ALA, and, as a result, Girls State thrived and grew with the nation.

Chapter 10

No Longer a Mythical State

During the period from the late 1970s through Frances Goff's death in September 1994, the Bluebonnet Girls State program reached maturity. Frances solidified and consolidated her leadership of the program while at the same time preparing for its future expansion and grooming a new generation of leaders. With growth came increasing complexity for the organization. In the mid-1950s, she ran Girls State on an annual budget of $13,500 and a staff of a dozen counselors and office personnel. By 1982, the budget had increased to $115,000, and, by her last year, that total had risen to $175,000. The size of the staff had tripled. The attendance at the sessions had also risen to 560 Citizens, very near the capacity of Texas Lutheran College to house them. In 1994, the total had grown to 586 women, the upper limit of Citizens that the facilities available could handle. During Goff's years as director and earlier as an assistant, 21,428 women attended Girls State and became part of a very powerful yet informal network of educated, middle-class women who possessed the skills and abilities to influence public policy in Texas.

Although the essential format of Girls States remained in place, Goff built on the educational mission of the program whenever possible. Coverage of judicial issues expanded, for example. In October 1986, Kappy Allen, an attorney and Citizen from 1976 who had returned as a counselor and Speaker of the House, recommended that "depending on your budgetary constraints" a judicial assistant position be created. She noted that the courts at Girls State now handled thirty-four court cases as part of the curriculum, many of which overlapped. A judicial assistant on the Education Staff could provide necessary advice and guidance for enhancing that aspect of the Girls State offerings.

Goff also devoted extensive attention to keeping the Girls State manual current. When Arliss Treybig, a former Citizen, became the chair of the American Legion Auxiliary Girls State Committee in 1985, Frances advised her that revision of the manuals should begin at once. "We need to write a letter to the state departments, enclosing a copy of what we have now with a request that they review it and make additions, deletions and/or corrections. I will also have some changes in the manual in so far as legislative procedure is concerned and some other sections, including the song part."

Treybig was a valuable ally in this process. She had been a Citizen in 1952, returned as Senior Counselor from 1958 to 1962, and then served on the office staff at Girls State from 1963 onward. "Really appreciate your good help, Arliss," Goff wrote, "for this is actually the first time to ever have anyone on the committee other than Jo [Hudson] who has been willing to assume some responsibility for part of all the paper work that goes on. It is a great help to me, and I appreciate your willingness to assume some responsibility." With her characteristic generosity, Goff told Treybig: "I do hope you will come to the [ALA] convention and remember if you can stand the mob you are perfectly welcome at 8406 [Lorrie Street, Goff's residence in Houston] not just for this convention, but anytime you need to be in the city."

Another educational concern that Goff pursued was an updated version of the 1977 film about Girls State. Working with Treybig during the summer of 1985, she first drafted a resolution approving the project for submission to the ALA convention. Despite delays in getting the document to the gathering, she won approval for the new cinematic record of what she and the Citizens were accomplishing. With that first step completed, Frances turned to the perennial matter of funding.

She tapped into her contacts in the worlds of foundations and politics. She wrote to Dr. Robert D. Moreton, the director of the John S. Dunn Research Foundation and an old friend from M. D. Anderson in March 1986. The foundation had helped her in 1977. "We will be most grateful if the Dunn Foundation can again look favorably upon our request for all or part of the necessary cost." Another source whom she approached was George Strake Jr. of the Strake Foundation. Strake was a rising figure in the Texas Republican Party and a frequent participant in Girls State sessions. In a July 1986 letter, she laid out her plans for the film project and asked for the foundation's assistance. The 1977 film had been a highly successful public relations enterprise, and she anticipated equally gratifying benefits from her current venture. "We are now in the process of raising funds for this purpose. We would be indeed grateful if the Strake Foundation could once again give us monetary support." Strake noted on the standard form letter reply: "Frances—We will do what we can. George."

Despite the fund-raising donations that she did achieve, a lack of funding slowed progress on the film's production in 1987. One of the donors wrote to her in October 1987 to find out "what plans you have made concerning the updated film on Bluebonnet Girls State." The money that had been allocated to the American Legion Auxiliary for the film would have to be used soon, or the donor would direct that it be spent for some other purpose. Goff told her "that we are hoping to be able to get our film [at?] the next session of Girls State. . . . There are many things pending in which I am involved until the end of the year. I will not be able to pursue the film project until that time." Because they could not do any filming except during a Girls State session, they had to forego shooting in 1987. "However, we are making every effort to complete the project in 1988 if at all possible."

Further delays put off the film for yet another year. In April 1989, she approached Professor Horace Newcomb of the College of Communication at the University of Texas at Austin, and sought his assistance. "In 1977 we made a 16 mm film of Girls State. We used some of your students. We are doing a videotape this year. I will appreciate an opportunity to discuss with you the possibility of seeking assistance from your department in the production of this undertaking." Finally, after all these delays and obstacles, the videotape was produced in 1989.

To Goff's dismay, the hard work that had gone into the Girls State video did not translate into sales from the Citizens. Noyes M. Willett, who helped her market the film, told Frances in April 1990 that "I too am surprised that the video sales were not stronger. Sales of the audio product have steadily diminished over the years, a fact that I had thought to be partially because we were dealing in an ever more obsolete media. I had thought that the video would do better, particularly since the price was so reasonable. Ah well, my crystal ball was never too clear." That the memories and experience of Girls State did not prove more of an attraction to the former Citizens made Goff "a bit sad," as she noted on the copy of Willett's letter that she sent to her godson and colleague on the video project, Jeff Rasco.

The task of managing the financial affairs of Girls State was another responsibility that Frances Goff assumed and one that brought her frequent concerns and nagging problems over the years. Girls State provided medical insurance coverage for the Citizens during their stay in Seguin. Claims were paid to the attending physicians and the Williams Drug Store in the town. In

1987, however, the insurance company accidentally paid the claims to the Citizens themselves rather than the local firms and physicians. Goff had to write and apologize for the mishap. "Needless to say," she added in her letter, "I have recommended to our insurance agent that we no longer use this particular carrier."

Revenues for the Girls State program came from the official pins that the store sold to the Citizens. When Goff realized in 1987 that their current supplier was, in her mind, providing a limited selection of pins at high prices, she arranged better choices for the young women. Goff located a firm that promised to "definitely supply you with the good quality found in jewelry made only in the USA." The change was duly and promptly made.

Despite her careful supervision of all aspects of the Girls State financial activities, Goff sometimes received criticism for her performance in this area. In December 1987, the certified public accountant in charge of overseeing the affairs of Girls State and the American Legion Auxiliary wrote to the secretary-treasurer, Collette Lemley, to raise a number of issues about how the Girls State funds were being managed. He expressed concern that the Girls State store maintained a second money-market bank account in a Seguin bank with the funds unavailable to the Austin headquarters and with no department officer authorized to sign on the account. He also criticized the absence of an inventory list for the Girls State store. "We recommend that, for greater control, that [sic] all bank accounts be cut off at month end and that statements with canceled checks as well as all invoices or invoice copies be sent to you. A department officer should be authorized to sign on all bank accounts." The copy of this letter that Goff kept in her papers exhibits her frustration with the charges that the accountant raised. She underlined his sentence about the bank accounts and noted in the margin that the signatures were "on file at the bank." She also bristled at a charge that she did not maintain a careful inventory of the store's stock from year to year.

In response to these comments, Goff wrote Bea Fuhrman, the department president of the Auxiliary, in July 1988 to say that "my position does not involve the operation of the store as it is strictly under the committee. However, they asked me to discuss this matter with you to seek a resolution." Members of the Girls State Committee stayed late at the close of the Girls State session that year to iron out these financial issues. Frances told them that the "account in question has proven very helpful in order to pay our vendors promptly and have all of our bills settled by the time the Girls State session is over." With her usual command of the evidence, she documented how the Girls State Committee had established these procedures in previous meetings. Goff was scrupulous in her handling of the Girls State accounts, and no hint of scandal or misappropriation of funds occurred during the four decades that the Girls State funds were under her supervision.

A recurrent vexation for Goff and her program were complaints about Girls State. In March 1989, for example, a member of the Auxiliary from El Campo, Delores Valigura, wrote to say that the her local school "seems to think [Girls State] is their program." Valigura insisted that "I really feel that the members of the Auxiliary should have a little say in the selection of the Girls State Citizens. This letter will probably not make any difference to you and the Girls State Committee, but I wanted to let you know my feelings on this subject. I feel that we are being pushed out in the cold and it is an ALA program." Frances explained that the local units decided how many girls they could sponsor. Then the schools selected an initial pool of applicants. Finally, the unit would make the choices about which of the candidates were chosen to attend Girls State.

A year later in July 1990, Terry E. Priestap of Laredo said that no one from that city had been chosen for Girls State "because no one at the local level of the ALA was interested in coordinating the program . . . and because no one at the state level took the interest to make sure that the coordination was being done. . . . This occurrence speaks poorly of the sense of responsibility of your state organization." Goff patiently reminded Priestap that "the State Office of the Department of Texas Auxiliary does not go out into the community to solicit the Citizens—this is the responsibility of the local units *NOT* the State Office. We are sorry Laredo was not represented this past year. This responsibility lies totally upon the local units and not the Department."

The Girls State program also encountered the changing cultural demands of the 1980s as it applied to potential Citizens with physical disabilities. In April 1984, Lloyd Doggett, a Democratic state senator and U.S. senatorial candidate, complained to Wanda Konkel, the Auxiliary's department president, about the wording of the waiver of claim form for Citizens. That document stated that "Delegates must be physically fit and able to participate actively in this very strenuous schedule. Past experience dictates that individuals having physical impairments which prohibit them from keeping pace with the rigid schedule . . . ARE NOT considered physically fit." However, the program did endeavor to adjust for the needs of potential Citizens who had physical disabilities, as the ensuing negotiations with Doggett demonstrated.

Arliss Treybig wrote to Frances and the Girls State Committee in early May for advice about how to handle Doggett's complaints. No one in the Auxiliary knew who the girl in question was. "We do not know whether the girl herself is handicapped or her parents are just making a public reaction." Treybig remembered a phone caller who had asked for the name and address of the Department's president and the Executive Administrator. That seemed to be the origin of the matter. In any event, Konkel advised Doggett that the Girls State program had resolved such medical problems involving potential Citizens on "an individual basis after consultation with the Girls State director, the girl's doctor, and the parents." The failure of the parents to approach the Girls State Committee or Frances Goff with their question had precluded an amicable resolution of the matter within the program itself. It is not clear from Goff's records whether the young woman attended the 1984 program or not.

Throughout the 1980s, Frances continued her crusade to restructure the Girls Nation Program. A proposal for overhauling it remains among her personal papers. She wanted Girls Nation Junior Counselors selected much as Bluebonnet Girls State Junior Counselors had been chosen since the early 1950s. In her proposal, however, she added that "Junior Counselors should be selected based upon their service to their own Girls State program. Prior to invitations being issued, the director and/or staff of Girls Nation should clear the invitation with the Girls State Director."

Frances advocated a youthful Girls State National Committee to shape policy. She carefully specified that this committee would not wield major influence over the revamped Girls Nation Program. "The Junior Counselors should be the only ones who deal directly with Girls Nation Citizens. It has been proven that it takes youth to lead youth. Is it necessary that members of the committee be present and members of the Girls Nation staff?" From the outset, Goff wanted to avoid the situation she had faced originally in Texas where members of the Girls State Committee exercised undue influence over the shape of the program.

The procedures for connecting Girls Nation delegates with representatives from their home state members of Congress concerned Goff. Not all of the delegates had the same exposure to national politicians. Goff argued that while "it is quite important that all of the Citizens of Girls Nation visit their national capital," another approach might prove more fruitful for all those at Girls Nation. She proposed that "two or three prominent cabinet members or members of congress could come to the campus of the university where Girls Nation is being held and speak to all of the Citizens and conduct a question and answer period which would be much more beneficial for the total complement." What had worked so well in Texas ought to operate with equal efficiency nationally.

Her greatest criticism of Girls Nation lay with the disregard of parliamentary procedure in the mock sessions of the Senate in which the Citizens participated. She wanted a former Girls Nation participant placed on the staff as president of the Senate who could make the sessions as realistic as possible. "The girls that have attended Girls State," she wrote, "and have a highly structured legislative program are extremely dismayed by the lack of protocol, procedures, and the lack of ability of the presiding officer."

While Goff had very real concerns about the conduct of Girls Nation, she also worried about the inconsistency between the various Girls State programs throughout the nation. Goff encouraged the ALA to assist with Girls State and ensure a uniform program. The problem arose because the American Legion Auxiliary convention spent far too little time on Girls State and far too much time on planning for Girls Nation. It angered her that the national Girls State Committee could talk for hours about Girls Nation without out a single mention of Girls State. "Many of the Girls State directors need help with their programs and this is an ideal time to have a general discussion with questions and answers relative to some of their problems." For Goff, "this pre-convention committee meeting should think of the thousands of girls throughout the states and not dwell on 100 in the Girls Nation program." Despite these recommendations, the Girls Nation and Girls State procedures did not change that much. Frances Goff had to content herself with letters such as the one she received from Miriam Junge, the national secretary of the ALA in January 1989. Junge told her that "it goes without saying, you have an outstanding Girls State Program in Texas. While it is not a known fact, I pushed hard to get your gals on the Girls Nation Staff for I knew they would do an outstanding job." In the end, the Girls Nation program did not receive the benefits of Frances Goff's reforming instincts that had done so much for the Texas version.

The tensions that sometimes characterized Goff's relations with the national organization emerged in one episode during the early 1990s. The *National News of the American Legion Auxiliary* printed a feature entitled "The Women of Girls State," which claimed that "to commemorate the Girls State/Girls Nation program the National News started a search for past participants." Goff was pleased to see Ann Richards mentioned in the article, but the neglect of other Texas women, and the focus on the Girls State programs of the Midwest irritated her. She wrote on her copy of the article: "Texas was never '*searched.*'"

Throughout the 1980s, the strength of the Bluebonnet Girls State program rested on Frances Goff's ability to provide a distinguished roster of

Cyndi Taylor Krier (on left) at capitol with a Citizen, 1989. *CN 08911. Courtesy Texas Bluebonnet Girls State, Center for American History, University of Texas at Austin.*

speakers from state government and politics for the Citizens at the annual meetings in Seguin. Just as she had used her links with the Democratic party in the 1950s and 1960s, Goff now supplemented these contacts with her friendships in the resurgent Texas Republican Party. She still exchanged comments with her old GOP friend Jack Cox, who told her in a July 11, 1978, letter that he had "thoroughly enjoyed our political conversations. You are most astute and your opinions have always meant much to me."

The speakers at Girls State thus reflected Goff's eclectic political beliefs. In 1981, for example, she had Karl Rove, a staff member of then-governor

William P. Clements and a Republican consultant, speak to the Citizens about the role of political parties and their place in American government. "I'm not saying you should vote a straight ticket, I'm just saying that political parties are the ones who decide what candidates will be voted on. They are essential to the democracy that we have."

Republican women served as role models for the Citizens. Rita Clements, the state's First Lady, spoke in 1981. She stressed that "the women of our nation make up 52% of the population and I think we have not only the opportunity, but also the obligation to participate more fully in working for the betterment of our society." Other GOP females who appeared in Seguin included Carole Keeton Rylander, a former Citizen from 1956, former mayor of Austin, and future Railroad Commissioner; and Cyndi Taylor Krier, a Republican member of the Texas Senate elected from San Antonio in the mid-1980s. Krier became a regular speaker in the late 1980s and early 1990s.

Goff's closest tie within the GOP hierarchy in the state was with George Strake Jr. He spoke several times during the 1980s. As he told the Citizens in June 1983: "Right now the world is in desperate need of leaders. Everyone who has reached the top has had some setbacks. They eventually succeed because they are persistent." Accordingly, he advised his audience to "start walking with, talking with, and listening to all sorts of people, instead of paying attention to titles or political parties."

Strake made frequent appearances at the Girls State sessions during the 1980s. When he could not come, as happened in 1986 because of a conflict with the GOP state convention, he asked Goff whether she could "give me a rain check for future years because this is one of the events which I enjoy the most?" For her part, Goff congratulated Strake when he decided to remain as chairman of the Texas Republican Party. "I hated to hear that you were stepping down and am glad you changed your mind. You have done so very much with the party and I would not like to see it fall into hands that would let all of your hard work be in vain." She assured him that he would be welcome at future sessions. "Please know that your name has not been taken off our speakers list." In 1988, she invited him back once again.

Goff had known George Bush since the 1960s when he emerged as a force in Houston and Texas Republican politics. After Bush's presidential inauguration in 1989, she sought his participation in the Girls State program. She commended him "for the excellent Cabinet and other officials you have selected. I hear many favorable comments relative to your appointments, even from some die-hard Texas Democrats." She recalled his previous visits to Girls State in the 1960s and early 1970s, and invited him and

First Lady Barbara Bush to speak in Seguin to the 1989 session. Although Goff assured him that security at Texas Lutheran College would not be a problem, her legendary powers of persuasion could not induce the White House to have an incumbent president appear at Bluebonnet Girls State.

On one point involving the state and national politicians whom Goff enlisted to speak at Girls State she was most insistent. When the inauguration ceremony for the Citizens elected to Girls State offices occurred in the rotunda of the state capitol, she expected the actual officeholders to fulfill their commitments to attend and to support the program. Nothing made her angrier than to have public servants embarrass their office and themselves in front of the young women who were learning about government service.

In the early 1990s, this issue became acute. The 1991 inauguration ceremony proved humiliating for Frances because several officials failed to show up at all and did not send suitable representatives. Frances apologized to an official on the lieutenant governor's staff whose calendar backed up because of the delays. Despite her careful checking in advance "to reconfirm their appearance," the individuals were not there. "I have never in all my years with Girls State experienced such a lack of 'those who were supposed to be there.'"

Even those who showed up did not always cooperate. State Treasurer Kay Bailey Hutchison departed early in 1991 because of these delays, leaving her Girls State counterpart alone. As Goff's successor as Girls State director, Connie Bridges, recalled the general problem, "everything that Frances Goff did was up to par and it was done correctly. So Frances expected the same in return. When you have an official that would agree to come and participate, and they didn't live up to the bargain, Frances didn't like that. . . . It was like Girls State was her baby, and if you did something against that it was not easy to erase." With her usual grace, Goff wrote a tactful letter to Hutchison apologizing for the difficulties and stressing that events had gotten beyond her control once the other officeholders had absented themselves.

Renovation of the state capitol during these years posed other problems for Goff's ingenuity. She had to scramble to find alternate sites for the inauguration and the mock session of the state Senate in 1992. The nearby First United Methodist Church served as a place for the inauguration, and she improvised other locations for the Citizens to hold their legislative sessions. Having a former Citizen as the governor of Texas helped Frances Goff achieve her goals. Ann Richards interceded with the State Preservation Board to secure use of the capitol rotunda in 1992. "The Texas Girls State program

Maryana Iskander and Ann Richards. *Photograph by Mark Prochnow. Courtesy Round Rock* Leader.

has used the rotunda for over four decades, and I request the use of the rotunda for this program," the governor declared.

The changing dynamics of the American population had its effect on Girls State, and Frances Goff responded with tolerance and insight to new circumstances. In 1992 one of the delegates to Girls Nation was Maryana Iskander, an Egyptian by birth who became a naturalized U.S. citizen in 1989 and was chosen as a Rhodes Scholar in 1996. Elected governor of Bluebonnet Girls State, Iskander wanted to run for Girls Nation president. The policy of the American Legion Auxiliary prohibited non-native born Citizens from serving as president or vice president of Girls Nation. Frances concluded that it was a silly rule since it prevented a talented woman from seeking a high office. Goff and Connie Bridges attended the 1993–1994 National Girls State Conference to argue for a policy change. When the ALA officials contended that the letter of the American Constitution should be followed and that naturalized citizens should be ineligible, Goff replied that the Constitution also barred anyone under the age of thirty-five from serving as president. Yet that circumstance had never blocked a seventeen-year-old Girls Nation delegate from becoming president of the organization. Thanks to the urging of Goff and Bridges, the Conference recommended that each state department design a more flexible policy to accommodate unique situations.

In the early 1990s, Frances summed up her work with Girls State in a speech to ALA. She told the Auxiliary of her forty-three years with the program and her thirty-eight as its director. "In spite of the continued progress of Texas Girls State, there have been many upheavals, misconceptions, vicious rumors, and consternations during these years created by those not familiar with the operation and purposes of Girls State." She explained her efforts to "remain positive, objective, and dignified in the resolution of all of the adversities thrown in the way of Texas Girls State progress." She celebrated the triumphs of Girls State in Texas. "Through these years we have grown, and are known throughout the United States as having the most highly structured educational program in the nation. This could not have been accomplished without total objectivity by the devotion of the fine, young women who are former Citizens of Girls State." Frances made veiled criticisms of the ALA for their sometimes unwelcome interference into the internal workings of the program. "Many times [former Citizen volunteers] became discouraged because of accusations and untruths." Frances, though, recognized the help she had received from the ALA. "We have also had very loyal and faithful members of the auxiliary. Their continuity of service and hard work has proven their devotion and support." The long-serving director praised her fellow volunteers for the success of their efforts. "We are held in high regard at the national level and many states seek information relative to our program so they might add to theirs."

Throughout the remaining years of her life Frances received numerous commendations for her public service. Arliss Treybig coordinated an effort in 1985 to have Frances nominated for a Freedoms Foundation award, which was a national honor unlike the numerous state and local awards she had already earned. In 1985, Frances told Arliss that: "I appreciate what you are doing relative to my nomination for the Freedoms Foundation award." Administered through Valley Forge, the awards for individual achievement as described in a brochure went for "contributions supporting human dignity and the fundamentals of a free society." Frances was a 1985 winner of the Valley Forge Honor Certificate for Individual Achievement from the Freedoms Foundation.

After Frances received a Distinguished Service Award in 1986 from Texas Lutheran College, Theos Morck wrote her and declared, "you really deserved that award for what you have done for the young lady Texans during the past 35 years. That is a tremendous contribution you are making by sharing your talents of leadership with that fine group. Keep it up." For her volunteer efforts Frances Goff was inducted into the Texas Women's Hall of Fame in 1986. That same year the national ALA honored her work with Girls State. She had been an honorary lifetime member of the Texas ALA since 1971.

For a 1991 ceremony honoring Frances on her seventy-fifth birthday, Lloyd Bentsen delivered a written tribute to the woman with whom he worked on the internship program for Girls State in the 1970s. "Frances Goff will always be remembered for her leadership in the Bluebonnet Girls State program and her service to University of Texas M. D. Anderson Cancer Center. The contributions you have made have been many, and we appreciate all that you have done for your community and the state of Texas."

In July 1991 at Frances Goff's seventy-fifth birthday party, Girls State alumni discussed plans for a Frances Goff Scholarship Fund at the Lyndon B. Johnson School of Public Affairs. By October, the first $10,000 had been raised and donated to the school in what became an on-going effort to raise money. Ninety percent of the income generated from the endowment went to student awards with the remaining 10 percent reinvested. The scholarship funded summer internships in the governor's office to students with a 3.5 grade point average, demonstrated financial need, and who had attended Girls State. In May 1992, Texas Governor Ann Richards told Frances that the LBJ School internship was "a great idea!" The governor observed that "an LBJ School student will be invaluable to implementing the goals and programs of this office. I appreciate your generosity and I look forward to having an intern help us during the summer months." By 1993, the fund grew to $80,000 after Frances and others made key donations. The University Board of Regents provided a matching grant of $20,000 to boost the endowment to $100,000.

In a 1986 interview Frances reflected on her work with Girls State. She told a reporter for the Houston *Chronicle* that she was not a feminist. "I've worked in a world where I've been competitive with men. I believe in equal pay for equal jobs but bra burnings, demonstrations—no." She pointed out the uniqueness of her role with the program. "For the last 25 years, I am the only person who has direct contact with Girls State who has not been a Citizen of Girls State." Her love for the program never abated. "I enjoy it

Goff, Trahan, Bridges, early 1990s. *CN 08952. Courtesy Texas Bluebonnet Girls State, Center for American History, University of Texas at Austin.*

too much—I enjoy the girls too much. I enjoy seeing the change in them and then beginning to have a respect for the city or state or country."

In the last few years of her life, Frances turned more and more authority for the program over to a group of women who spanned the various Girls State generations. Mary Ellen Trahan, the associate director for education, and Rubyrae Phillips, the talent director, had been Citizens in the 1950s and had been involved with the program on and off ever since. Ann Doan and Elaine Ginsburg, Citizens in the 1960s, worked with the office staff. Connie Bridges and Tammy Broz, Citizens from the 1970s, helped as associate directors. This transfer of power would not have been possible had it not been for Frances's initial farsightedness in creating an institutional memory for the program. Indeed, the informal network of former Citizens provided the talent to take over responsibility for the program's success.

After Frances's death in 1994, Connie Bridges became the Girls State director. Arliss Treybig believed this collection of talent would sustain the program. She said of the new director: "Connie fools people, I think, because she's small and kind of soft spoken, but she is a very strong person, very intelligent, a very capable young woman. They all know the program, they know what's involved. They know what Frances has done, what she's tried to do. They wouldn't have stayed with it all these years if they hadn't believed in it." Treybig asserted, "we want to think it's going to be continued. Otherwise, what Frances did would have been wasted for the future, and we don't want to believe that."

After Frances's death, Connie Bridges reflected on her skills as a teacher. "I think the first thing I felt was, I just said 'Frances don't leave me,' because she had been so much to all of us. Of course, Girls State means a lot to me and it has been a big, big part of my life. But Frances Goff in so many ways has been my teacher in so many areas. . . . She emulated that for all of us, and was a role model in so many different areas, other than state government. For the staff as well as for the Citizens, it was always an on-going learning process." Bridges knew the future of Girls State was secure as long as its leaders remained true to Frances's goals for the program. Her philosophy indicated that Arliss Treybig's concerns as to whether "the spirit of Frances is strong enough in those people who are more directly involved that it will continue and not falter" were for naught. The spirit of Girls State lived in the lives of the 20,000 plus women who profited from exposure to Frances Goff and her finely tuned program. Indeed, when women like Ann Richards attained state and national prominence, Girls State was "no longer a mythical state."

Chapter 11

"The Shoulders to Stand On": Frances Goff and Ann Richards

The political triumphs of Ann Richards, first on the local level then as state treasurer and governor, proved more visibly than any other evidence that Girls State was "no longer a mythical state." Her relationship with Goff had grown over forty years. Ann Richards first came to Frances Goff's attention in June 1949 when, as young Ann Willis, she attended Girls State as a Citizen. Neither woman knew that the relationship would grow over the years as the younger woman climbed to the pinnacle of Texas politics. According to the June 21, 1988, edition of *The Bluebonnet*, Ann Richards told the Citizens at Girls State that "As you grow older, there will be people you will recall that helped you grow the way you are." She then asserted Frances Goff was that person for her.

Goff realized the extent of Ann Willis's capabilities and tapped her for service in the newly created junior counselor role. Willis volunteered at Girls State during the early 1950s. The June 18, 1952, edition of *The Bluebonnet* indicates the extent of Ann Willis's activities. When a mock session of the Girls State House debated whether women should serve on juries, Willis, for the sake of argument, took the negative. *The Bluebonnet* reported that "Miss Ann Willis, Junior Advisor and debater for Baylor University, put up a stiff argument against the resolution, stating that women are not emotionally stable to qualify for the position. . . . The lively debate was heightened when Miss Willis stated that the author of the bill was proof that women should not be on the jury as she could not stand the pressure of continual questioning." Willis's tactic worked; the Citizens plunged into heated debate and passed the resolution anyway.

As the demands of family increased on her time, Ann Richards moved out of the direct Girls State orbit in the mid-1950s. She graduated from Baylor

To Frances who started me on this career many years ago. I love you. Ann 1987

Frances Goff and Ann Richards in an embrace. Richards wrote: "To Frances who started me on this career many years ago. I love you. Ann, 1987." *Photograph copyright Ave Bonar. CN 08968. Courtesy Frances Goff Papers, Center for American History, University of Texas at Austin.*

University in 1954 and married David Richards, her high school sweetheart. The couple moved to Austin so he could attend law school. They then settled in Dallas where Ann Richards went to work raising four children and volunteering with progressive, Democratic causes. In 1969, she and her husband returned to Austin. However, Ann Richards's life eventually led into the public arena. As such, her contact with Goff increased. Richards later described Goff as "the base, she was the shoulders to stand on. You knew that no matter what you might ask of her, within reason she would do it. She was a constant support system." This support system included the informal Girls State network of former Citizens, which in many ways came full circle with Richards's political success. Exposure to the political process had, in fact, produced a rising political star.

Richards explained the evolution of her political relationship with Goff. From her entry into local politics as Travis County commissioner in 1976, Richards made an annual pilgrimage to Girls State as a featured speaker, but did not talk with Goff regularly. Richards explained that "when I ran for Treasurer, Frances really didn't figure into it, except that she was always very much out there to try to help. Once I made a statewide race, she wanted the American Legion to be aware of me, and she wanted them to be proud of me." Goff also made sure Richards nurtured a relationship with the M. D. Anderson community. The involvement of the mentor with the protégé increased dramatically when Richards ran for governor. "In the Governor's race though, Frances was hands-on. It was simply amazing. She raised money. She brought me to meet people and them to meet me. She did a good job of it too." Richards also detected a much more progressive, feminist-oriented attitude in Goff dating as far back as the early to mid-1980s.

Goff's patronage of Richards demonstrated a seeming anomaly in her political outlook. Known among friends as a staunch conservative, she now worked for the liberal Ann Richards. When talking of Frances's support for Ann Richards in the 1980s and early 1990s, Anne Hodges Morgan explained that friendship and personal loyalty had much to do with Goff's apparent move away from the Republican Party. Morgan later commented that Goff "is programmatically liberal. Frances is a compassionate, I would say she's a social liberal and a fiscal conservative." Furthermore, Pat Mathis suggested that "as Ann [Richards] began to advance in her career, I think Ann became a point of pride to Frances, just as Barbara Jordan or any of the rest of us who were extraordinarily successful were. Frances feels legitimately that she played a part in all of that." Thus the politics of personal friendship more than the politics of ideology dictated Goff's actions. To do otherwise could have been interpreted as a repudiation of her star pupil from years earlier.

Richards usually talked to Frances about the major political events in her life and the Democratic National Convention in 1984 was no different. The Texas state treasurer was a member of the Texas delegation to the National Democratic Convention. She wrote Goff about that historic occasion and the impending selection of Geraldine Ferraro, then a Democratic congresswoman from New York, as the vice presidential nominee. "The historic value of this political year is growing every day. Can you imagine a woman Vice Presidential candidate? I never thought change would come about as quickly as it has. I appreciated your nice note. Speaking at Girls State will always be a highlight of my year. Who knows, one of these young women may follow the path that congresswoman Ferraro is pioneering into the White House!"

Four years later, Richards wrote to Goff about another National Democratic Convention. In 1988, she had been selected to give the keynote address. She thanked Goff for her support and spoke of her trepidations about the talk ahead. "Knowing that I have the support and help of so many friends like you helps in understanding this overwhelming task. I appreciate your taking the time to write to me. Once again, I loved being part of Girls State." It was at this convention when Richards gained national fame. Her remarks proved the high point of an otherwise difficult year for the Democrats. She electrified party stalwarts with the now famous remark about the difficulties women face in public life. She assured her audience that women were capable of any challenge they might face; then Richards quipped that Ginger Rogers had done everything that Fred Astaire had, only backwards and in high heels.

As Richards's fame increased so did Goff's efforts to help her career. In the aftermath of Richards's performance, Goff lobbied unsuccessfully for her inclusion on the speakers' program at the National Convention of the American Legion in San Antonio that fall. Goff told Miriam Junge, the national secretary for the ALA, on January 9, 1989, that "You will recall I mentioned she would have been an excellent speaker for the National Convention in San Antonio but for some reason there was not a spot for her. Needless to say, you perhaps saw her deliver the keynote address at the National Democratic Convention in last July."

The 1990 gubernatorial campaign proved a decisive example of Goff's commitment to Richards. In this contest, Goff supplied money of her own, access to contributors who might otherwise not donate to a Democrat, contacts with the medical community in Houston and the American Legion/American Legion Auxiliary, and moral support. Richards's note to Frances from the 1990 campaign declaring "Dear dear Frances—What would I be today without your generosity and inspiration—probably ironing and sweeping" indicates the depth of affection between the two women.

Connie Bridges remembered that when Ann Richards decided to run for governor Goff sat her down and gave her advice. Goff advised Richards that "you need to be ready to be hit hard on some issues, and your family needs to be ready. Those are the things that you need to sit down and talk over with your family to see if they're willing to do that, if they're willing to support you." Goff worried how an unscrupulous candidate might twist Richards's recovery from alcohol abuse for political gain. Goff cared most of all how such charges might affect Richards personally. So she took on the role of protector and counselor.

Bridges speculated that "the great thing about Frances is that Ann could rely on her. Here was a person who has had her life, she's had her success. She's not looking for any favors, she's not looking for anything from Ann. Can you imagine how nice it would be to be Governor of the State of Texas and know there's a friend out there, a person that has probably a wealth of information, a wealth of advice, and would give all of that to you freely and not expect anything in return."

Despite Goff's admiration for Richards, her decision to support her candidacy took courage because it meant a sharp break from her past political allegiances. Bea Ann Smith recalled the extent of Frances Goff's political courage. In 1989, Goff went with Smith to the Hyatt Regency for Ann Richards's announcement party for her 1990 race for governor. Goff told Smith that "these are the people I've been lambasting for years, what am I doing here. I'm not comfortable. Who are these people," she asked. Smith assured her that "It's okay, they are not going to bite." Smith praised Goff's "courage to go ahead and do that, and . . . to make that switch, and make that commitment to Ann Richards. Go to friends who were not likely supporters and win them over. I think she had so much personal courage."

Richards needed a friend like Goff in 1990. That race proved one of the most bitter in Texas political history. From the Democratic primary all the way through the general election, Richards faced personal attacks on her own life and her record as state treasurer. By the second week of February, Richards warned Frances to "Hang on—it's going to be a rough ride." Later that month, Richards thanked Goff for her financial donations since money was key to getting out the vote for the March 13 primary. This portion of the campaign proved trying for Richards since the other Democratic contenders, especially Attorney General Jim Mattox, turned the race into an extended exercise of character assassination with charges of alcohol and drug abuse. Richards penned an addition to her note: "I hate this garbage part of the campaign and it is due to get worse. I love you and thank you. A."

Richards found herself in a run-off after the ballots were counted for the Democratic primary. She polled 39 percent of the vote while Mattox had 37 percent. The run-off promised another grueling month of campaigning. One week after the Democratic primary, Richards sent Goff a standard thank you for her financial contribution, but added a personal note at the bottom. "I never get home early enough to call you. I'm on the road constantly now and I think we're OK but run-offs are terribly unpredictable. We've simply got to get *our* vote out. I love you and thank you!" Richards succeeded in getting her vote out, and she defeated Mattox handily by a margin of 57 percent to 43 percent, or 640,995 to 481,739.

With the primary season over, Goff worked even harder for Richards. The race for November proved even more difficult because the GOP challenger, Clayton Williams, a wealthy man with oil and gas, banking, and telecommunications investments, could rely on his personal coffers while positioning himself as a political outsider. Goff was appointed a member of Richards's statewide finance council for the general election in 1990. In early June 1990, Richards thanked Frances for "making it possible for me to speak at M. D. Anderson." The gubernatorial candidate penned in: "Frances, Sorry this note is so long getting to you but I have really been swamped. Lots of serious policy speeches, travel and chasing the almighty dollar. I loved doing the M. D. Anderson event. Who do we know in the medical center that will give or raise money? Love you, Ann." Despite the press of the campaign schedule, Richards made her annual visit to Girls State. After the visit she sent Frances a note thanking her for another financial donation, with a handwritten addition about Girls State. "It was good to be at Girls State although I had a *long* day and was tired so I fear I was not at my best."

During the midst of the campaign, Frances Goff sought an invitation for Richards to speak at the 1990 ALA convention. For Goff getting Richards before the socially conservative ALA was crucial to broadening her base beyond more traditional Democratic constituencies. While plans for Richards's appearance seemed firm in May 1990, by the time for the summer gathering opponents within the ALA had blocked the invitation. Goff therefore gave a speech to the ALA meeting in which she praised Richards personal and political accomplishments. She told of the nearly unanimous approval of the Girls State Citizens that year for Richards. Goff cited the comments of several young women in her remarks: Richards "'made us realize any of us could be whatever we wanted. She was inspirational. She said it was okay to be a woman and a leader.'" Another Citizen stressed that "'she set forth an attitude that was pro feminist yet did not kill the ideal for the family.'"

Goff had little patience for those who opposed Richards. She told the ALA that "the few of you who have criticized, objected, and threatened to embarrass this speaker have not only defied the principles of Girls State but also the ALA, and have put your stamp of discouragement on future Citizens to follow their motivation and aspirations." Speaking of the move to prevent Richards's appearance at the ALA, Goff stressed that "I realize my remarks do not apply to the majority of our membership. But if the shoe fits wear it and if it's tight I strongly recommend you not only enlarge the size of your shoe but your vision, your tolerance, your integrity, and exemplify your belief in a democratic society. Do not give with one hand and take away with the other."

That summer Frances did arrange for Richards to speak at the American Legion Department of Texas Convention. Richards sent Goff a note of appreciation in early August. "Another 'Thank You' to Frances! You do so much for me and this campaign—I am grateful for your continued support. I loved being with you at the American Legion Convention. It was a tough group and having you with me gave me the lift I needed."

Goff's political activism on Richards's behalf reached new heights in August 1990 when she wrote a long letter to the editor of the Houston *Post* and criticized the tone of Clayton Williams's campaign for governor. Goff summarized her long history of employment with the state of Texas and her familiarity with political campaigns. "I realize there are times when distortions and misrepresentations are made. This year it is horribly overdone. The thing that perturbs me about the Republican Party and their candidate for governor is there seems to be no knowledge, regard or consideration of the Constitution of the State of Texas, Statutes of the State or Texas, or the Legislature of the State of Texas." She was especially upset with the way Williams misrepresented the functions of the state treasurer's office.

Williams's comparisons of the interest earned by the state treasurer's office with the Teacher Retirement System, the Employees Retirement System, the Permanent School Fund, and the Permanent University Fund irritated Goff. The Republican nominee asserted that the management of Richards's office compared unfavorably with the way that the latter offices functioned. Yet Goff countered in her letter to the editor that "I have always heard of comparing apples and apples and oranges and oranges but never have I heard of comparing a *grape* to a *watermelon*, which in my opinion is exactly what this recent attack signifies." She noted that retirement systems and the school funds maintained long-term investment structures while the treasurer's office operated short-term investments.

Thinking back to her days as budget director, Goff declared that "when one has given as much time to the state as I have it is frightening and shocking for those seeking office to treat their responsibilities lightly, which indicates their lack of understanding of our government and needs. Government needs to be understood and nurtured as one would nurture a child." Goff explained that this was her first letter to the editor. She castigated Williams, a man of significant financial resources, for his "attempt to buy . . . a state." Goff explained that "having devoted and dedicated the major portion of my life to the State of Texas and my country, I feel very strongly about what happens."

Her anger about Williams and his campaigning style persisted. When Frances read an article in the October 10, 1990, edition of the Houston *Chronicle,* her frustration with the Republican gubernatorial nominee that year increased. The *Chronicle* reported on Williams's recent remarks at M. D. Anderson Hospital about the greater productivity of private-sector workers over government employees. While praising the Anderson employees, Williams made the overall assessment that "a private professional contractor will nearly always do a better job than an in-house public employee." The following day, Goff sent a letter to the *Chronicle* expressing her outrage at Williams's charges. "As a 53-year employee of the State of Texas I highly resent and take exception to [Williams's] statement. . . . There are thousands of great state employees throughout our government. They should not be subjected to this gubernatorial candidate Williams lauding the private sector employee over those of the State of Texas."

Her actions that fall were not limited to letter writing. In the September and October issues of the *Legion Times,* a monthly publication of the American Legion and the American Legion Auxiliary, Frances Goff arranged for a political advertisement on behalf of Ann Richards. She raised $3,400 from former Girls State Citizens to pay for the advertisement, which summarized Richards's background, her involvement with Girls State, her support for veterans' issues, and asserted: "Vote for Ann Richards November 6 and help Texas soar to new heights." The fine print declared that the page in question was a "paid political advertisement by former Citizens and staff of American Legion Auxiliary Bluebonnet Girls State in appreciation of Ann Richards's motivation, dedication and continued interest in Girls State."

Yet the advertisement sparked controversy. Jimmy D. Lemley, the department adjutant for the American Legion, wrote to Laurey Tutor, the secretary for the ALA, that "our office has no problem with this advertisement, however, the words 'American Legion Auxiliary' should not have been used. Our office has, and is receiving telephone calls from Legionnaires who are very upset with the words in this ad of 'American Legion Auxiliary'. Of course, our organization cannot endorse any candidate for any public office." Lemley said that the next issue of the *Legion Times* would contain a retraction. He asked that Tutor explain to the ALA membership that this organization did not pay for the ad. "This will help my office, if you can explain this mistake to your members." The uproar over this advertisement proved another example of Frances's long-term efforts to broaden the horizons of the ALA and the Legion.

The efforts of Goff and many other Richards's supporters ultimately proved successful. Richards prevailed that November by a margin of 49 percent (1,925,670) of the vote to Williams's 47 percent (1,826,431); minor candidates garnered the remaining ballots. For Goff and many others associated with Girls State, Ann Richards's victory in November 1990 offered validation for much of what they had undertaken over the years. Frances saved newspaper clippings in her personal papers about Richards's political triumph in November 1990. Furthermore, Tammy Edwards, a sophomore at Stanford University and the 1988 governor of Girls State, wrote to Goff in November 1990 after Ann Richards's victory over Clayton Williams. She declared: "Girls State showed me that with a strong sense of self, a desire to serve, and a little help from my friends, nothing is impossible, but I think that Governor Richards's victory really gave that belief a concrete base and immense reinforcement."

After Richards's election, Goff maintained close ties with the new governor. In July 1991, the governor thanked Goff for becoming an executive board member of the Governor's Leadership Council. Throughout the Richards administration, Goff continued her activities as a fund-raiser and liaison for the governor. Goff maintained lists of Harris County supporters for the governor in her personal papers. She also had several pending lists of gubernatorial appointments that were marked for her attention. Indeed, Frances played a key role in directing Richards's attention to talented women who might play a role in state government. Frances even worked with her out-of-state contacts to improve the governor's national visibility. Richards selected Goff to work with the Governor's Commission for Women and the selection of candidates for the Texas Women's Hall of Fame.

Goff prevailed in securing an invitation for Richards to speak before the ALA in 1991. Because of a special session of the Texas legislature, Governor Richards was unable to make the scheduled visit to the American Legion Auxiliary's convention in July 1991. Instead she sent a short statement apologizing for her absence: "As I told the American Legion Convention last year, I am where I am today, at least in part, because I was fortunate enough to participate in Girls State. . . . Because of your devotion to young people—and the hard work of Frances Goff—I learned early that as Citizens, we have an obligation and an opportunity to serve our country. I still go back to Girls State every year, and I still believe what I learned there." The ALA invited her again in 1992 and commented that "We are very proud that you recognize our Girls State program as being an important factor in your career and we hope it will be possible for you to share your experiences as Governor of our state and let us know what we can do to assist in THE NEW TEXAS."

In fact, Goff helped Richards cultivate alliances with many of Houston's wealthy Republicans. On April 8, 1992, for example, she arranged a dinner at the Governor's Mansion for some Houstonians whom she knew through M. D. Anderson and her Republican Party ties. Among the guests were Richard and Cindy Burns, active supporters of the Williams campaign until the end of the first primary. Richard Burns, a Houston attorney, was, according to the resume of guests Goff prepared for the mansion dinner, "on the Finance Committee when Clayton made the announcement 'now I'm going to buy me a state' at the River Oaks [Country Club]. Dick told him to look for another Finance Chairman. Both became very active in run-off and general election." Another couple on the guest list was Chris and Claudia Sangster. Goff made this observation of Claudia Sangster: "A very attractive and smart young woman — a graduate of University of Houston Law School—she would make a good regent—and yes—she was at Girls State—outstanding Citizen and went to Girls Nation."

Frances played a key role in a June 18, 1992, Houston fund-raising event for the governor. She served as a sponsor for the $1,000-a-couple cocktail party for Ann Richards at the home of Jack and Laura Lee Blanton. The Blantons were wealthy Houstonians; he was a long-time donor to the University of Texas and a member of the UT Board of Regents. As a sponsor Goff agreed to give or raise at least $5,000 for the governor. Richards remarked "this event is the first major fund-raiser to take place outside of Austin since I took office more than a year ago. Your willingness to help raise money for this event sends a powerful message, as it enables me to fund an ongoing political office and its activities."

Goff also took an interest in one of the major policy initiatives of the Richards years. Public school finance dominated the state's headlines for much of the early 1990s. Goff had a copy of "The Governor's Good Schools Plan" in her papers, which was a talking document with quotes from the governor and a breakdown of the plan. Frances made a financial contribution to the Save Our Schools campaign in March 1993. This campaign involved three ballot initiatives reforming public school finance. Despite a massive media push, the plan failed at the hands of the electorate on May 1, 1993.

Goff raised a significant amount of money for Ann Richards in 1990 and proved a vital force in her election effort. Had it not been for the decline in her health, she would have done so again in 1994. Anne Morgan recalled

Ann Richards speaks at Girls State, 1990. *CN 08946. Courtesy Texas Bluebonnet Girls State, Center for American History, University of Texas at Austin.*

that "she would bring busloads of prominent Republicans to Austin to have dinner with Ann Richards, and of course Frances would be there as the tie." However, Goff became involved in one unintended event from the reelection campaign. In 1994, Richards made her traditional appearance at Girls State and the event turned into a political controversy that summer.

After her election as county commissioner for Travis County in 1976, Ann Richards returned year in and year out to Girls State, from 1978 onward. Billee Lee, a staff member, recounted that "the girls love her. . . . She's always their favorite." Myra Hester, another staff member, said: "I think the reason why is Ann gets right down to their level. She says 'Girls, I want you to know this. When I'm through, I'm not going to leave anything out. If there's something you want to know about my life, my personal life, I'll be happy to tell you.' She starts out, she tells about raising her children alone, about her divorce, about everything. She doesn't hold back. I think that's what they like. She's so natural."

Richards gained this praise because she spoke honestly about the life experiences women might face. The June 22, 1994, edition of *The Bluebonnet* reported on her remarks from that year: "you can change jobs, colleges, and you can even change the town you live in, but you are all you've got for the rest of your life. . . . The only measure that counts is the one you make for yourself." She encouraged the Citizens to ask three questions of themselves. "Who are you? What do you want to do with your life? And, what do you want to be? . . . It's hard to keep your hair shiny and swishy and be assertive at the same time."

Although Richards had been delivering this message to the Citizens of Girls State for more than fifteen years, two circumstances made the occasion controversial. First, it took place in Austin rather than Seguin because of the demands of the governor's schedule. Second, because it happened during the gubernatorial campaign, reporters heard it for the first time. The Republican contender George W. Bush depicted the speech as anti-family and anti-woman. He told the press he was "amazed" at her speech. The Houston *Post* reported on June 22, 1994, Bush's statement that "this is not the message Texans want their leaders to give our daughters or sons."

The political flap outraged Goff, and she summoned her failing energies for one last effort on behalf of her political protégé. Frances mobilized Citizens and former Citizens of Girls State to defend and explain the context of the governor's comments. This became her final campaign before her death later that summer. She encouraged a newspaper letter-to-the-editor writing campaign. For example, Amanda Matthews wrote a letter to the Dallas *Morning News* that appeared on June 29, 1994. "Richards captured thoughts that had been formulating in my mind and put them into words—thoughts that told me to be myself, believe in myself and to depend on myself. She sacrificed

Frances Goff and Ann Richards in golf cart at Girls State, 1990. *CN 08945. Courtesy Texas Bluebonnet Girls State, Center for American History, University of Texas at Austin.*

herself to media attention so that she could talk to us straight, just as she always has at Girls State."

Frances herself issued a press release that defended Richards's speech. "The Governor educates young women about the realities that they might encounter in life and urges them to be self confident. It is exactly at these critical teenage years that girls' confidence levels begin to drop, affecting their outlook on the future. The Governor tells young women that believing in themselves is a tool critical to their success. Few have the courage to talk honestly and openly with young people about these important lessons. This is exactly the reason that the Governor has been so effective at reaching and motivating young women." Despite Goff's exertions, the episode hurt the Richards campaign, in part because of the inadequate press coverage of her previous statements at Girls State and the ignorance of Texas reporters about Goff's role in state affairs.

After her defeat, the former governor reflected that Frances "wanted me to speak because I said outrageous things. Not that there was anything wrong with what I said. It was just that no one else said [it to] them. I've always liked to say out loud what everyone is saying behind their hand. I think I made the same speech for about twelve years, and Frances always loved that. She loved me to tell those girls you cannot count on someone else taking care of you. And no one else wants to tell girls that. Everyone wants to tell boys that."

The longtime friendship between Goff and Richards existed on many levels and involved a significant degree of mutual respect. However, the Girls State connection was the strongest bond that the two women shared. Individually and collectively, the Girls State program had provided so much for each of their lives. Ann Richards remarked on her visits to Girls State as a speaker since she entered the political realm that "I told myself for years that I was going for the girls but in truth I think I was going for Frances. It meant so much to her. It was as if our presence in public office validated her existence." However, Richards's appearances at Girls State also gave back a tremendous gift to the next generation of Texas leaders. The respect and admiration that the Citizens felt for Richards permeated their evaluations of Girls State. Thus the Goff-Richards friendship gained in sentiment as Richards's career gained in prominence. Their individual successes seemed a confirmation of the work they had separately done.

When Frances Goff died on September 15, 1994, Ann Richards was still Governor of Texas and in the thick of a losing race for reelection. Yet Goff literally went to her grave proclaiming her feelings for Richards and the campaign then in progress. Goff had arranged for an "Ann Richards for Governor" bumper sticker to be affixed to her coffin; in September her wishes were carried out at the state cemetery in Austin. This last act closed out Frances Goff's important contributions to the political career of the most famous and influential of the former Citizens of the Girls State program.

Chapter 12

"This Grand Lioness of a Woman": The Legacy of Frances Goff

W hen Frances Goff died, her memorial service was as much an opportunity to mourn the loss of an old friend as it was to commemorate the life of an influential woman. Several hundred people gathered in Houston for the occasion and shared their memories. A few months after her political mentor's death, Ann Richards reflected that "it was just this great joy and pride that she had, this grand lioness of a woman, who had nurtured and nudged these kids out of the pack, and they had survived and done well." The image of Frances as a protector loomed large throughout her life. She often used the example of her experiences and outlook as the basis for advice she gave friends and acquaintances.

Frances had a prayer known to Citizens of Girls State as Goff's Prayer. This statement of faith characterized Goff's attitude toward life:

Lord, Thou knowest better than I know myself that I am growing older and will someday be old. Keep me from the fatal habit of thinking I must say something on every subject and on every occasion. Release me from the craving to try to straighten out everybody's affairs. Make me thoughtful but not moody; helpful but not bossy. With my vast store of wisdom, it seems a pity not to use it all—but Thou knowest, Lord, that I want a few friends at the end. Keep my mind free from the recitals of endless details . . . give me the wings to get to the point. Seal my lips on my aches and pains. They are increasing and love of rehearsing them is becoming sweeter as the years go by. I dare not ask for grace enough to enjoy the tales of other's pains but help me to endure them with patience. I dare not ask for improved memory, but for a growing humility and a lessening cocksureness when my memory seems to clash with the memories of others. Teach me the glorious lesson that occasionally I may be mistaken. Keep me reasonably sweet; I do not want to be a saint—some of them are so hard to live with—but a souring old person is one of the crowning works of the devil.

Give me the ability to see good things in unexpected places and talents in unexpected people. Give me the grace to tell them so. Amen.

This prayer was reprinted from year to year in *The Bluebonnet* and helped explain how Frances succeeded in working with women younger than herself.

Throughout her life, Frances developed her own sayings for handling life's challenges and problems. These sayings, known as "Goffisms" or "Francesisms," sound familiar to anyone who worked with Goff in the state legislature, at M. D. Anderson, or at Girls State. One of her favorite adages— "you pay for the ground you stand on"—grew from her belief that people have a responsibility to work and contribute to the betterment of society. "You can give 'em books and give 'em books, all they do is chew the corners" reflected her frustration with people who sell themselves short. A friend said that "with Frances there was always one more hill to climb, one more test to pass." Indeed Frances believed one should never give up. She also believed that "if you want to get the job done it doesn't matter who gets the credit."

Connie Bridges remembered that the memorial service for Frances included a review about the "Francesisms" most common at Girls State. She explained that "it was all of the things, part of the traditions of Girls State, and things that reminded us [of her]." At this service commemorating her life, they talked about the values that were most important to Goff. Frances stressed each year at the orientation for counselors at Girls State: "we don't allow gossip at Girls State." Connie recalled that Frances would say "if you walk around and you don't get it out in the open, and don't get it solved, it will cause problems. Don't allow it to fester. Get it out in the open, don't allow it to fester." Bridges recalled one orientation session where Frances left out the part about "letting it fester." This omission upset some of the counselors who remarked among themselves: "Frances didn't say the part about, when she was talking about gossiping, she didn't say the part about don't let it fester." Bridges speculated that Frances made this policy work because of her own personality. "She was the type if she had something to say to you, she was going to say it."

Goff was willing to support her friends not only with words of advice and encouragement but also with her actions. Perhaps the ultimate example of Goff's devotion to her friends was the large number of people whom she watched die, often at her house. If a friend were sick, Frances made sure that person received the best care available in Texas, which often meant bringing them to M. D. Anderson. She learned who the doctor was and she observed the treatment process. Anne Hodges Morgan explained that after the patient's release from Anderson "you have to go and stay at her house while you recuperate. She'd never tell you this. Half the time she has somebody there getting over some kind of surgery, some kind of chemotherapy, some whatever. I've known her to look after people just when she's been exasperated beyond belief with them because she thinks that's what she ought to do, that's what she does, that's how she treats people." If the disease was one that did not permit a return to good health, Frances then stayed with her friends until they died.

In July 1992, Ann Richards thanked Goff "for keeping an eye on my friend LaRue Ward and for giving us an update now and then." Virginia Bailey was another friend whom Frances cared for in the last years of her life. When Bailey was diagnosed with cancer, Miriam Junge, the national secretary of the American Legion Auxiliary, wrote to Goff in January 1989. "Sorry to hear about Ginny. My thoughts and prayers are with her. She is also a special friend. It must be comforting for her to know she has someone as loving and as trusting as you by her side. Take care of yourself dear one. Know we love you and treasure your friendship."

Perhaps the most poignant example of Frances's compassion came from her care for a young woman with an eating disorder. When a former Citizen called Frances about the condition that had sent her to a treatment center, the young woman was nervous about the reception she would receive. Frances responded with love and compassion for the pain of the disease this person had suffered. The woman wrote back to Frances and declared "I had my discharge ceremony today from my treatment and had a hard time reading a complete sentence of your letter with a dry eye. I can't thank you enough for your kindness and love. . . . I want to tell you what a big role you and Texas Girls State have played in my finding the strength to want recovery. . . . The loving and encouraging family I have with Girls State and the work I have done with the girls showed me that there was much more to life than I had allowed."

Frances's compassion also made her a person who felt very seriously about the activities she undertook. Frances believed so intensely in the merit of the Girls State program that she truly hated to lose a Citizen to homesickness. The first defection occurred at a session during the late 1950s or early 1960s. Arliss Treybig remembered the incident because the homesick Citizen was in her city. "We finally let her go home. It was hard for Frances because, as she said, 'I've never lost one before. I've never lost one before.' She had to let her go." Since the activity level was so intense for the ten-day session, Frances expected every participant to approach the program with enthusiasm and energy. There was no time for boys, dances, phone calls home, or anything else that distracted from the purpose of Girls State. When someone had difficulty making the same commitment she herself had made, it troubled Goff.

Citizens and former Citizens found in Goff a friend for life. Valerie Lowrance wrote to Frances in December 1985 and told her that she could not come to Girls State in 1986 but asked that Frances remember her for future sessions. "The friends you make there are friends for life; an elite group who share a unique experience that always unites them and binds them. Wherever I go I run into a Girls State family member." Lowrance recalled that as a freshman at the University of Texas one of her suite mates in the dormitory was Tami Magee, a woman with whom she had attended Girls State and who had gone to Girls Nation. "Tami and I have found that we continue to run in to friend from Girls State on campus and it always makes the vast university seem a little smaller, a little warmer, and a little more like home."

Indeed the Girls State experience was one many women wanted to remember and relive. Girls State proved a transforming event for many of those who went through the program. One former Citizen remarked that the program brought her out of her shell. Her father remarked after she got home that she now spoke more than she had previously in her entire life.

Going back to Girls State became an even bigger honor for some than the initial selection as Citizens. Marsha Grissom remembered that her wedding conflicted with the timing of Girls State. As soon as the wedding was over, her husband commented that "Marsha, I've got to take you down there. I just can't handle this. It's like you hit a real lull. You need a pump up." When they got to Girls State and Frances met Don Grissom, it was like a reunion between two old friends. After one session of Girls State, Arliss Treybig wrote to Frances in July 1985 that "I enjoyed my two weeks with MY GOOD FRIENDS." Girls State Citizens became an extended family for Frances, and when they began their own families through marriage and childbirth Frances usually played a key roll as would any close family member.

Frances routinely opened her home to her Girls State friends. While some of the former Citizens believed a phone call out of the blue might have been an intrusion into Frances's busy world, others visited and dined with her regularly. In a conversation about Frances, Dale Coe Simons remembered that "I never got to sleep in a bed; I was always on the couch." Anne Morgan responded that "at least you didn't have to share a bed with Frances; I used to have to do that."

Frances Goff often saw to it that some Girls State alumni gained employment at M. D. Anderson. Dale Simons recalled the week she returned from her honeymoon. She had plans for moving and settling into her new apartment. Her new husband answered the phone and Simons heard him saying that "yes, certainly she'll be there eight o'clock Monday morning." Goff had hired Simons to work in the mailroom at M. D. Anderson Hospital. When Simons recalled this story with some other Girls State alumni, the gathered women remarked in unison: "everyone starts in the mailroom!"

Frances Goff's devotion to her Girls State family emerged in many outlets. One demonstration of her commitment to the young women she shepherded through the Girls State program appears in the file, which is several inches thick, containing letters of recommendation that Frances wrote on the behalf of her adopted family. Barbara Shell's April 1992 letter to Goff indicated her gratitude for Goff's help in securing her appointment to the Texas Board of Physical Therapy Examiners. "I believe the real accomplishment is in gaining your support and confidence." In addition to women aspiring to careers ranging from education to medicine, somewhere within the file may be a letter from a future U.S. senator or Texas governor. Frances had great skill in recognizing talent. One former Citizen, Nancy Ohlendorf, described Frances Goff's uncanny knack for watching people to see what they were capable of doing.

A writer for the June 17, 1986, edition of *The Bluebonnet*, declared that "although Miss Goff has received many awards, perhaps the most satisfying rewards are those of friendships that combine to form a vast network of 'builders in a band' throughout the state. The directors, in fact, often refer to each other as 'family.'" The writer asserted that "Miss Goff certainly believes in learning and working but she feels that friendships such as these are a vital part of Girls State. She encourages the Citizens to venture out and make new friends—'friends for life.'"

The love and friendships begun at Girls State inevitably carried forth into the remainder of the year. Women from the Houston area began getting together throughout the year. Eventually, the women who devoted their time and energy to Girls State decided they needed to hold regular retreats. Part of the plan included having a place to go and relax for a few days at the end of Girls State before the long drive home. As Arliss Treybig remembered: "The last weekend we're so tired, we've lost so much sleep. I was afraid to drive home because I was afraid I'd fall asleep trying to get home the next day."

Long-time American Legion Auxiliary activist Maureen Martin and her husband owned a log cabin in the vicinity of Trinity, Texas. They invited

Frances with her dog Ziggy. *CN 08966. Courtesy Frances Goff Papers, Center for American History, University of Texas at Austin.*

Frances and other Girls State workers to use the cabin as a place to unwind. When Frances and company first started using the cabin there was no hot water. The rustic conditions proved relaxing. A river nearby provided opportunities for fishing. The retreats, referred to as Trinity, began among the Girls State volunteers but continued because of their friendships not because of any great attempt to plan for future Girls States. As Treybig remembered, "it was just the time to see each other, and get to know each other, without having all of our duties and responsibilities of Girls State. . . . If we do our job, we don't have a lot of time to visit. They are such neat people, such fun people, and then we think we don't even have a chance to talk very much, and to get to know each other" at Girls State.

Frances relied on the get-togethers at Trinity to solidify the core of the Girls State volunteers. She usually scheduled a meeting at Trinity in the fall and another in the spring. Marsha Grissom, a former Citizen of Girls State from 1963 nicknamed "Grochelle," recalled her first invitation to Trinity. Frances called her out of the blue one day and asked, "Grochelle, what are you doing?" Grissom, who had not talked to Frances in twenty years, responded: "obviously, just waiting for you to call, what can I do for you?" Frances invited Grissom to the next Trinity meeting. When she arrived, Grissom told Goff: "Hello, Miss Goff, it's so nice to see you." Frances then replied, "Goddamnit, Grochelle, call me Frances." Grochelle complied: "Yes, Ma'am, Frances."

Despite the many friends Frances had, she also had a personality which sometimes intimidated people. Billee Lee recalled that fear of disappointing Frances was a strong motivater. Lee remembered that Frances had two dogs that she often brought with her to Girls State. The two dogs, Poco, a Chihuahua, and Gigi, a straight-haired, black poodle, were constant companions for Goff at Girls State. "If we were doing something we thought she might not want [us] to, or being just not really right or something," Lee recalled, "we'd hear the pitter patter of little feet, and boy did we straighten up fast. Frances, she just gave off that authority."

Anne Morgan observed that "Frances appears to be a very serious person. She's about as serious as a junebug." And indeed there was another side to that atmosphere. Frances understood how to put together a program that combined the serious study of government with the fun-loving side of life. The balance between education and recreation proved central to the bonding process that drew the young women together into the informal Girls State network. Part of Goff's brilliance had something to do with that old phrase "all work and no play." Frances Goff had an infectious sense of humor. It was easy for people to say things like "she was the only person who slept at attention" or to call her Colonel as a nickname behind her back because they knew she enjoyed a good laugh. Indeed, the role of Girls State in the lives of thousands of Texas women cannot be understood without looking at the lighter side of the program.

So along with the serious side of learning how politics and government work, there were numerous planned and unplanned humorous aspects of Girls State that contain an equally important message: never take yourself too seriously. In the mid-1950s, Frances was lecturing on state government one evening when someone on the staff learned that some boys had sneaked into the grounds. The rest of the staff and counselors were all out chasing them and trying to get them out. Someone called the police on these local boys who were out having a good time. Those outside requested that the Citizens remain in the auditorium in assembly until the male intruders were removed. As Frances finished her lecture, the talent staff led the young women in a song or two. In the meantime, Frances learned of the disturbance and remarked to the Citizens that: "well girls you know you might be wondering why we kept you so long in here, I am just going to be honest with you." She then told them about the boys. The talent staff started playing some background music on the piano such as the Lone Ranger theme. Frances and company made a melodrama out of the event. The more she talked the better her story got. As a result everyone enjoyed what could have been an unpleasant event.

Sometimes humor combined with the serious side of running Girls State. At one point Mary Ellen Trahan gave Frances a foam cooler cover for beverage cans with the saying "you can't start off the day unless you have a good toad." The saying implied that no one is ever perfect, and at some point everyone must answer for their mistakes. It also spawned a huge humorous reaction to Frances's high standards for Girls State. Connie Bridges told the story of how she and other staff members remarked, "oops, had a toad today," meaning that Frances had questioned some aspect for which they were responsible. Frances never called someone down out of anger. Instead, actions of this sort were strictly to improve the program next time.

In one particular episode, a mouse had gotten into one of the dorms. The Senior Counselor reported it and Connie arranged for its removal with Frances none the wiser. In October or November, Connie got a call from Frances. Frances asked Connie why she never mentioned the mouse. Connie's response was a questioning "Ma'am?" as she wondered what on earth was going on. After Connie remembered, Frances asked again why she

Girls State Citizens perform a skit parodying "Othello" in 1962. The main cast included Kathy Retz as Othello, Lucy Yoder as Desdemona, Lyn Martin as Amelia, and Arliss Treybig as Iago. *CN 08964. Courtesy Texas Bluebonnet Girls State, Center for American History, University of Texas at Austin.*

never told her about it. Connie explained that with the mouse removed she thought the problem had been solved.

Frances related that the Texas Lutheran College president heard about the mouse episode, for the first time, when the Seguin delegate to Girls State gave a talk about her experiences at one of the local service clubs. The president immediately called Frances and explained that he had been embarrassed to hear such a story in a public environment. Of course Frances didn't know either, thus sparking the call to Connie. As Connie told it, she learned an important lesson about management from that experience. Frances explained that the person in charge must know of problems to aid in dealing with the public. Bridges summarized that Frances's high expectations were what made Girls State run so well. "She kept us all in line. Our fear of her I think a lot of times kept us on our toes. But it wasn't fear from the standpoint of being afraid that you were going to be berated. . . . It was fear from the standpoint that we respected the woman."

The following year the staff took the toads even more seriously. To show there were no hard feelings resulting from the mouse episode, counselors and staff who had learned they should tell Frances everything responded in a very literal fashion with sticky notes declaring that they had gone to the bathroom and would be back in five minutes.

Often the humor at Girls State appeared spontaneously in response to events as they developed. One of Frances's favorite outfits at Girls State was white pants with a white Auxiliary shirt. The combination of white pants with

201

Rubyrae Foster's skit, "Fanny Goof." Ruth Ann Hicks joined Foster on center stage while several counselors assisted the act. Left to right in background: Jackie Howard, Dianne Ferrell, unidentified counselor, and Iona Kubby. *CN 08955. Courtesy Frances Goff Papers, Center for American History, University of Texas at Austin.*

white shirt against her white hair was striking. In fact some staff members nicknamed her the "White Tornado" because of her hair. One year at Girls State Frances put all these whites, along with her white underwear, in the washer together. Unbeknownst to her, a pair of red pants got mixed in with the whites. The whole wash, dainties and all, came out pink. The next day when she came to lunch, Frances was dressed, head to toe in pink. The staff questioned her: "Frances, they didn't have that shirt in the store in pink!" or "Frances, I didn't know you had bought pink pants this year." So she admitted what had happened, which was even more comical because Frances hated pink. White turned pink became a running joke that year.

On talent night one year, the Junior Counselors and the Senior Counselors put on a skit the "Wizard of Goff." It explained all the different things that can happen to the Citizens at Girls State. The House and the Senate became

Ann Richards and Frances Goff laughing at the Goffa, Goffa, Goffa skit in 1992. *CN 08904. Courtesy Frances Goff Papers, Center for American History, University of Texas at Austin.*

the "wicked witch" because that is what people fear the most. Frances loved the music in the movie the "Best Little Whorehouse in Texas" so the Senior

Counselors did a skit called the "Best Little Girls State in Texas" where they rewrote the show's lyrics to Girls State lyrics. The golf carts that staff members drove around the Texas Lutheran Campus quickly became "Goff Carts." The phrase, "So help me God," became "So help me Goff." Other skits poking fun at Frances included the "Fanny Goof" parody of Goff's efficient demeanor made famous by long-time talent director, Rubyrae Phillips. Since Frances worked for M. D. Anderson, people constantly asked if she was a nurse or a doctor. This incessant questioning prompted the "Are You a Nurse?" skit.

Perhaps the ultimate parody at Girls State was the creation of the Goffa, Goffa, Goffa Sorority. In 1992, some of the former Citizens who returned in staff roles wanted to do something that in their words would be "monumental, and at the same time would be fun, with just that special touch of Girls State class." Well in a brainstorming session someone said: "It's Goffa, Goffa, Goffa, Can we help you, help you, help you." The rest of the women said "that's it." As the plan emerged, eventually someone combined the theme of creating the Goffa, Goffa, Goffa sorority with a take off on the earlier pink underwear episode.

The staff members procured pink tee-shirts and took neon green material and affixed the letters GGG on the back. Since Ann Richards was coming to give her speech, someone decided it would be fun to initiate the governor into Goffa, Goffa, Goffa as an honorary member without telling Frances. While playing on the stereotypical dingy sorority girl, the staff members involved started singing: "Come along and be my Goffa girl, Come along and be my Goffa girl" to the governor. They then presented the governor with her Goffa, Goffa, Goffa pink tee-shirt. Frances's response was: "Hotamighty. How can you embarrass me like this. All these people are loving it." In reality Frances loved it too.

After dancing on stage and doing the Charleston, it was time for the formal initiation ceremony. With Rubyrae Phillips doing her Julia Child impression, she began the initiation by asking Ann Richards to repeat after me: "I, state your name." Well the staff had gotten to the governor in time, so Ann responded in kind: "I, state your name." Frances hooted with delight at the stunt. The Citizens that year sat with their jaws dropped wide open as the staff members acted in absolute parody of the ultimate authority figure for their program: Frances Goff. Yet the humor and jokes played an important role at Girls State. Frances knew the program would not succeed without balance. She realized people have to laugh to release the stress and tension that builds up with hard work. As a result of this balance between study and play,

Ann Richards receiving her Goffa, Goffa, Goffa T-shirt in 1992. *CN 08903. Courtesy Frances Goff Papers, Center for American History, University of Texas at Austin.*

the bonding process for each year's Citizens took place on many different levels and strengthened the ties that were formed for ten hot summer days each year.

Throughout her life, Frances Goff worked with numerous political leaders in Texas. Although never a household name, she was "well known to people who matter." As such she herself became a mentor to thousands of women. Anne Morgan told her on one occasion that "you were a role model before anybody knew what a role model was." She explained that Frances let young women know that they could succeed if they wanted to. Frances never pretended that it would be easy for women to compete in a man's world. She told the many Citizens of Girls State that they would have to better in order to compete, but she also made it clear that women were better. Morgan recalled that Goff did not tell women to avoid more traditional choices:

"Frances never ever disparaged or in any way belittled the traditional role of the mother, the wife, and the family, she never did. Frances likes the gentlemen, and so she always thought it was important to be married and have a family and all that." In the end, Frances conveyed to the 21,428 women who attended Texas Bluebonnet Girls State the variety of choices before them and she encouraged these women to find the path most suited to their interests and talents.

Frances's friends and former Citizens of Girls State worked hard to repay their debts to the woman who had been an inspiration for so many individuals. The people who knew her best wanted her to receive the recognition they believed she deserved. As a result of their efforts, her resume grew long with a listing of the many awards she received throughout her life. She gained the Matrix Award from Women in Communication's Houston chapter. Goff was a life member of the ALA and a statewide honorary member of Delta Kappa Gamma Society International. The American Legion recognized her contributions with the National Commendation Award. Finally, a scholarship program was endowed in her name at the University of Texas at Austin's Lyndon B. Johnson School of Public Affairs.

When she died in September 1994, Frances Goff had in her seventy-eight years made the most of her opportunity to play a key part in the public life of Texas. From her days as a legislative secretary in the 1930s to her role during the Ann Richards era of the early 1990s, Goff had exerted a constructive influence on state politics. She had contributed to the growth of Texas medicine through her work at M. D. Anderson Hospital under R. Lee Clark. Most of all, as the director of the Bluebonnet Girls State program for more than four decades, she had been a positive example to generations of Texas women about the need for public involvement in the political affairs of the state. One of these varied careers would have been significant. To have managed all three in the course of a single lifetime was a testament to the passion and commitment that impelled Frances Goff to make a special place for herself in the modern history of Texas.

Texas Bluebonnet Girls State, 1952–1994

Dates	Location* and no. of Citizens	Governor	Girls Nation Delegates
June 16–22, 1952	TSD, 325	Ruth Parker	Sharon Jones, June Konolle
June 15–21, 1953	TSD, 325	Jean Manning	Grace Morrow, Barbara Terrell
June 21–27, 1954	TSD, 327	Mary Mead	Mary Mead, Corky Marcus
June 6–15, 1955	TSB, 360	Wanda Sumrall	Wanda Sumrall, Emma Hernandez
June 7–16, 1956	TSB, 360	Sherry Stewart	Pat Mathis, Mary Decker
†June 10–19, 1957	TSB, 360	Anita Erb	Anne Hodges, Diana Duke
June 11–20, 1958	TSB, 360	Marilynn Wood	Mary Ellen Trahan, Judy Haddon
June 10–19, 1959	TSB, 400	Ginger Mead	Ginger Mead, Betsy Williams
June 8–17, 1960	TSB, 400	Jean Faulkner	Virginia Kennedy, Bea Ann Smith
June 14–23, 1961	TSB, 400	Mary Ann Wycoff	Mary Ann Wycoff, Carole Brennan
June 13–22, 1962	TSB, 400	Sara Speights	Janet Matthews, Bette McCall
June 12–21, 1963	TSB, 402	Margaret Morrow	Susan Riley, Helen Kitchen
June 17–26, 1964	TSB, 402	Brenda Cook	Dianne Ferrell, Nancy Pritchard
June 16–25, 1965	TSB, 402	Marjorie Wilhelm	Janice Salzman, Judy Matthews
June 17–26, 1966	TSB, 402	Rebecca Best	LaNan Hooker, Bobby Specht
June 14–23, 1967	TSB, 402	Debra Brock	Debra Brock, Sue Oliver
June 11–21, 1968	SEU, 420	Sherry Clements	Marquerite Wilhelm, Beverly Fecel
June 10–20, 1969	SEU, 450	Ester Chavez	Patti Holton, Linda Marable
June 16–26, 1970	TLC, 456	Melissa Weaver	Steffi Sandler, Tanya Starnes
June 15–26, 1971	TLC, 450	Glenda Brown	Kim Ferraro, Claudia Batten
June 13–23, 1972	TLC, 512	Kit Gauthier	Beverly Brewer, Jane Montgomery
June 12–22, 1973	TLC, 517	Theresa Dunlap	Cathy Patton, Roxann Rippamonti
June 11–21, 1974	TLC, 515	Connie Grusendorf	Mary Ann Wissell, Mikie Collier
June 10–20, 1975	TLC, 515	Betsy Rowe	Susan Mengden or Duffy Valerius, Lena Guerrero
June 8–18, 1976	TLC, 517	Kappy Allen	Dawn Grass, Kappy Allen, Vicki Kemper
June 14–24, 1977	TLC, 560	Jennifer Weston	Jennifer Weston, Jennifer Bruch
June 13–23, 1978	TLC, 560	Debi Glover	Cathy Mengden, Silvia Orengo
June 19–29, 1979	TLC, 560	Janet Floyd	Emily Judin, Amy Karff
June 10–20, 1980	TLC, 560	Tammy Key	Mary Abbott, Lori Swann
June 16–26, 1981	TLC, 560	Monica Rosales	Dawnetta Lee, Lisa Zuniga
June 15–25, 1982	TLC, 560	Cindy Gay	Eva McGee, Nicole Willis
June 14–24, 1983	TLC, 558	Sonia Washington	Leanne Janke, Donna Jones
June 12–22, 1984	TLC, 573	Laura Bringol	Tami Magee, Stephanie Koury
June 11–21, 1985	TLC, 580	Lorinda Taylor	Kerrie Willis, Lisa Jones
June 17–27, 1986	TLC, 580	Stacey Floyd	Caroline Williams, Ellen Forman
June 16–26, 1987	TLC, 580	Sheila Hayre	Mindy Montford, Juli Simas
June 14–24, 1988	TLC, 580	Tammie Edwards	Tammie Edwards, Jennifer Pond
June 13–23, 1989	TLC, 580	Heather Stark	Ashley Chaffin, Emilee Whitehurst
June 12–20, 1990	TLC, 580	Tracy Edmondson	Stacey Riggleman, Lorin Looney
June 11–21, 1991	TLC, 586	Terri Williams	Smeeta Ramarathram, Elizabeth Stockton
June 16–26, 1992	TLC, 586	Maryana Iskander	Maryana Iskander, Annalisa North
June 15–25, 1993	TLC, 586	Alisha Force	Tania Krebs, Keri Worbington
June 14–24, 1994	TLC, 586	April Alford	Amanda Matthews, Annie Kersch

*TSD=Texas School for the Deaf   TSB=Texas School for the Blind
SEU=St. Edward's University   TLC=Texas Lutheran College

†In 1957 Frances Goff had no responsibility for Bluebonnet Girls State.

207

Note on Sources

Chapter 1
The Girl from Sixshooter Junction

Frances Goff set out the narrative of her early life in a series of oral history interviews with Nancy Beck Young and Lewis L. Gould in 1993 and 1994. This oral history, the original audio tapes, and Frances Goff's papers are now at the Center for American History of the University of Texas at Austin. Unless otherwise indicated, all information in this chapter is drawn from this material. Percy Goff's birth and the names of his parents are recorded in the General Register Office, London, England. The official birth record of Frances Elizabeth Goff, dated October 11, 1939, is in the Miscellaneous Volume, p. 205, Records of the County Clerk, Karnes County, Karnes City, Texas (hereafter RCC). Other biographical facts can be found in the obituary of Percy Goff, Kenedy *Advance*, March 1, 1945. Legal papers outlining a proposed divorce settlement between Percy and Ida Goff were filed in DeWitt County on May 4, 1909, and a copy was placed in Karnes County, May 13, 1909, Volume 38, pp. 304-305, RCC.

The Goff divorce suit is listed as *Grace Ingram Goff vs. Alfred T. Goff*, Case File B21321, Bexar District Court Records, San Antonio, Texas, and the quotations are from those documents. The murder charges against Jabbie Burrus are in the Karnes County District Court Records. Some of the biographical sources list Frances Goff as attending "San Antonio Business College." In the interviews she did in 1993, she carefully spelled out the name of Draughon's Business College, which is listed in the San Antonio telephone directory for the period when Goff was a student.

Chapter 2
Austin and the World of Texas Politics

In addition to the Frances Goff Oral History and the Frances Goff Papers, the major manuscript source for this chapter that is not mentioned in the text is the W. Lee O'Daniel Papers, Texas State Archives, Austin, for his speech about the Christmas orphans in 1940. The background of Texas politics in this period is examined thoroughly in George N. Green, *The Establishment in Texas Politics: The Primitive Years, 1938-1957* (Westport, Conn.: Greenwood Press, 1979). The legislative history and early years of M. D. Anderson Hospital can be found in the book that the hospital prepared to mark its initial two decades, *The First Twenty Years of The University of Texas M. D. Anderson Hospital and Tumor Institute* (Houston: The University of Texas M. D. Anderson Hospital and Tumor Institute, 1964). General background on public interest in cancer during the late 1930s and early 1940s is provided in James T. Patterson, *The Dread Disease: Cancer and Modern American Culture* (Cambridge: Harvard University Press, 1987). Some of the details about working in the Texas state capitol are mentioned in "Capitol times for capital woman, 77," *The Daily Texan* (Austin), May 9, 1995, in which Nell Hays, a secretary at the capitol in the late 1930s, reminisced about her experiences. Sen. James Taylor provided an interview in April 1993 that added insightful details about Goff's legislative career. That transcript and tape are part of the Goff Papers.

Chapter 3
Sergeant Goff

The information in the Frances Goff Papers on her wartime career is very complete, and she also talked about her wartime experiences at length in her oral history. A personal narrative that sheds light on what women such as Frances Goff encountered in the military is Anne Bosanko Green, *One Woman's War: Letters Home from the Women's Army Corps, 1944–1946* (St. Paul: Minnesota Historical Society Press, 1989). For the development of the Women's Army Corps and Oveta Culp Hobby's role, see Mattie Treadwell, *The Women's Army Corps* (Washington, D.C.: Government Printing Office, 1954). On the American Women's Voluntary Services, see Janet Flanner, "Profile: Ladies in Uniform," *The New Yorker*, July 4, 1942, pp. 21–29, and "Revolt in the AWVS," *Newsweek*, March 16, 1942, p. 46. On Love Field during World War II, see Al Hartung, "A Love Affair," *Westward: Dallas Times Herald*, July 15, 1984. Jerry Sadler's memoirs are (with James

Neyland) *Politics, fat-cats & honey-money boys: The mem-wars of Jerry Sadler* (Santa Monica, Calif.: Roundtable Publishers, 1984).

Chapter 4
R. Lee Clark and M. D. Anderson Hospital

Frances Goff talked extensively about her decision to move to Anderson in her oral history and in an interview that she did about the hospital in 1989 with Ann Rugeley, a copy of which is now in her papers. There is information about her appointment in the records of the University of Texas relating to M. D. Anderson at the Center for American History, and in the Allan Shivers Papers, Texas State Archives. For the selection of R. Lee Clark to head the hospital in 1946, see the President's Office Records, VF10A, Center for American History, University of Texas at Austin, which are very useful for the history of the hospital during the late 1940s as well. N. Don Macon, *Clark and the Anderson: A Personal Profile* (Houston: Texas Medical Center, 1976), is an oral memoir of R. Lee Clark that is helpful on his early life and medical training. *The First Twenty Years of the University of Texas M. D. Anderson Hospital and Tumor Institute* is also informative for this period. George N. Green, *The Establishment in Texas Politics*, provides the best background on the postwar political setting in which Frances Goff flourished.

Chapter 5
The Early Years at M. D. Anderson, 1951-1954

Frances Goff's papers contain an extensive file of correspondence and photographs about the dedication of M. D. Anderson Hospital's new building in 1954, and they have been used throughout this chapter. Her 1989 oral history interview discusses the early years of her career at the hospital, and she added some details in the 1993–1994 interviews. Goff also reminisced about this period of her life in 1976 in "'Ask Frances', they say at institute," *Houston Post*, October 4, 1976. The Goff Papers also contain biographical information on Virginia Bailey. The President's Office Records for the University of Texas at Austin are indispensable for the evolution of M. D. Anderson, as is Clark's published oral memoir, earlier cited. Goff's relations with the administration of Gov. Allan Shivers are outlined in the Shivers Papers, Texas State Archives, Austin. *The First Twenty Years* has good coverage of the dedication of the hospital as well.

Chapter 6
"Ask Frances": The M. D. Anderson Experience, 1955-1994

The Goff Papers were the main source for this chapter, along with her 1989 interview about M. D. Anderson Hospital. Two important letters assessing her contributions to the hospital in her papers are Robert D. Moreton to Avadne Montandon, August 28, 1985, and Charles LeMaistre to Avadne Montandon, September 27, 1985. "'Ask Frances', they say at institute," was again crucial for early details about her work. She also reviewed this phase of her life in "M. D. Anderson rep discusses building of cancer hospital complex," Beeville *Bee-Picayune*, January 19, 1981, clipping in Goff Papers. Betty Ford's comments about Anderson appeared in the Houston *Post*, October 3, 1976, and Shivers's role in the development of the hospital was examined in "M. D. Anderson lauds Shivers's commitment," Houston *Post*, May 27, 1979. "Cancer center leader Frances Goff dies," Houston *Post*, September 16, 1994, provided a brief review of her career with the hospital.

Chapter 7
"Youth Leading Youth": The Origins of the Bluebonnet Girls State Program

The Goff Papers provide crucial information on her early years with Girls State. Especially significant are the nearly complete run of Girls State manuals and *Bluebonnets* in the collection. A few key documents in the Allan Shivers Papers also demonstrate the lengths to which she went to attract high-profile speakers for the Girls State program. Her oral history provides key insights into her first years with the program. Oral histories with former Citizens and long-time Girls State volunteers also helped flesh out this chapter. See the Pat Mathis, Billee Lee and Myra Hester, Ann Richards, Ruth Moore, Anne Hodges Morgan, Rubyrae Phillips, Connie Bridges, and "Old Glories" including Jane Malaise, Nancy Ohlendorf, Dale Simons, and Marsha Grissom oral histories. See also the *Austin Gossip Digest* (July 1950); the San Antonio *Light*, August 19, 1951; *The Lone Star*, August 1952, May 1955; Austin *American*, June 5, 1947, June 2, 1948, June 13–17, 20, 1950, June 17–20, 1952, June 16–19, 1953; Austin *American-Statesman*, June 11, 1950, June 15, 1952, June 14, 1953. The article, "Girls State and Girls Nation," in *American Legion Auxiliary National News*, 65, no. 6 (75th Anniversary Issue, 1994), 20-21, has helpful background information on the founding of Girls State. Lilian Ware Tittle's book, *American Legion Auxiliary Department of Texas, A History: 1940–1950* (Austin: American Legion Auxiliary Department of Texas, 1955), has important details on the early years of Girls

State. The American Legion Auxiliary published a book, *Training Leaders for a Free Future: A History of Girls State, 1937–1957,* which is located in the Goff Papers and contains valuable background on Girls State. Finally Teresa Zunker's article, "In Goff We Trust," *Texas Historian,* 50 (May, 1990), 1–5, has unique insights into Goff's career with Girls State.

Chapter 8
The Maturing of Girls State

The Goff Papers contain important documents for exploring Goff's early conflicts with the ALA. see especially the Girls State manuals and *Bluebonnets.* The Jack Cox Papers, at the Center for American History, provide fresh sources for consideration of Goff's political activities in the late 1950s. The White House Social Files and the Lyndon B. Johnson Papers both at the Lyndon B. Johnson Library help with the story of integration. Goff's oral history provides key insights into the fight with the ALA and the integration of Girls State. Important oral histories are those with Pat Mathis, Pat Mathis and Anne Hodges Morgan, Ann Richards, Anne Hodges Morgan, Rubyrae Phillips, Bea Ann Smith, Arliss Treybig, and the "Old Glories." See also Goldie M. Bewley, *American Legion Auxiliary Department of Texas, A History: 1950–1960* (Austin: American Legion Auxiliary Department of Texas, 1963). Bewley's book contains veiled language indicating that the ALA supported the Goff ouster in 1957. Also see Mrs. Harold Johnson, *American Legion Auxiliary Department of Texas, A History: 1960–1970* (Austin: American Legion Auxiliary Department of Texas, 1973). For an indication of Clarence Manion's political ideas see Manion, *The Key to Peace: A Formula for the Perpetuation of Real Americanism* (Chicago: Heritage Foundation, 1951). For a history of Texas Republicans see Roger M. Olien, *From Token To Triumph: The Texas Republicans, Since 1920* (Dallas: Southern Methodist University Press, 1982), and John R. Knaggs, *Two-Party Texas: The John Tower Era, 1961-1984* (Austin: Eakin Press, 1985).

Chapter 9
Wider Horizons in the 1970s

For information on the move to Seguin and the Lloyd Bentsen Internship Program the Frances Goff Papers should be the first stop. Her papers are especially rich for the period after 1970. The Bluebonnet Girls State Scrapbooks should also be consulted. A related collection at the Center for American History, the Texas Bluebonnet Girls State Records, has much useful

213

information. The American Legion Auxiliary Department of Texas Files contained in their Austin office help with understanding of these years. Oral histories with former Citizens and long-time Girls State volunteers also provided needed background. See the Rubyrae Phillips and Arliss Treybig oral histories. Newspaper coverage of these years, especially the move to Seguin, is detailed. See the Seguin *Gazette,* June 18, 1970, June 25, 1970, the Seguin *Enterprise,* June 25, 1970, and the *Washington Post,* July 9, 1974. For the American Legion Auxiliary perspective see, Martha H. Collis, *American Legion Auxiliary Department of Texas, A History: 1970–1980* (Austin: American Legion Auxiliary Department of Texas, 1984).

Chapter 10
No Longer a Mythical State

The Goff Papers, including the Girls State manuals and the *Bluebonnets,* contain a wealth of information for study of Girls State in the 1980s and 1990s. The article from the *National News of the American Legion Auxiliary* is found within the Goff Papers. The Bluebonnet Girls State Scrapbooks and the Texas Bluebonnet Girls State Records should also be consulted. See the Rubyrae Phillips, Connie Bridges, and Arliss Treybig oral histories. Newspaper coverage of these years is helpful. See the Houston *Post,* November 24, 1991, and the Houston *Chronicle,* August 15, 1986.

Chapter 11
"The Shoulders to Stand On": Frances Goff and Ann Richards

For study of the Frances Goff–Ann Richards friendship there is a wealth of primary source information in the Frances Goff Papers. While closed to researchers at this time, the Ann Richards Papers at the Center for American History should prove rewarding to future scholars. Oral histories with former Citizens who knew the two women also provide insight into their relationship. See the Ann Richards, Anne Hodges Morgan, Pat Mathis, Connie Bridges, Bea Ann Smith, Billee Lee and Myra Hester oral histories. Newspaper coverage of these years is helpful. See the Houston *Chronicle,* October 10, 1990; Houston *Post,* June 22, 1994; and Dallas *Morning News,* June 29, 1994. Ann Richards wrote in her memoirs about Goff and Girls State. See Ann Richards with Peter Knobler, *Straight from the Heart: My Life in Politics and Other Places* (New York: Simon and Schuster, 1989). Sue Tolleson-Rinehart and Jeanie R. Stanley's book, *Claytie and the Lady: Ann*

Richards, Gender, and Politics in Texas (Austin: University of Texas Press, 1994), also contains helpful information.

Chapter 12
"This Grand Lioness of a Woman": The Legacy of Frances Goff

Everyone who ever attended Girls State or came into contact with Frances Goff through M. D. Anderson or Texas politics has some memory of that experience. This chapter is based on the recollections of many of the people who knew her well, including Ann Richards, Pat Mathis, Billee Lee and Myra Hester, Ruth Moore, Anne Hodges Morgan, Rubyrae Phillips, Connie Bridges, Bea Ann Smith, Arliss Treybig, Teresa Zunker, and "the Old Glories," including Jane Malaise, Nancy Ohlendorf, Dale Simons, and Marsha Grissom. Researchers should also consult the Goff Papers for issues of *The Bluebonnet*. For Goff's sayings, see her oral history.

Index

(Photographs are indicated by boldfaced page numbers)